Study Guide and Personal Explorations for
PSYCHOLOGY Applied to Modern Life: Adjustment in the 80s

WAYNE WEITEN

College of DuPage and Illinois School of Professional Psychology

Brooks/Cole Publishing Company
Monterey, California

Brooks/Cole Publishing Company
A Division of Wadsworth, Inc.

Printed in the United States of America

10 9 8 7 6 5 4 3 2

BF335.W42   158   82-4438
ISBN 0-534-01206-X

Subject Editor: Claire Verduin
Production Coordinator: Louise Rixey
Cover Design: Vernon Boes and Stan Rice
Typewriter Composition: Pat Polonus

To the Student

This book was assembled for you. It has two purposes. The first is to help you master the great volume of material covered in *Psychology Applied to Modern Life: Adjustment in the 80s*. The second is to help you to gain some personal insights from your work in this course. These two purposes are reflected by the fact that the book is divided into two parts. The first part is the *Study Guide*. It is this part that is intended to aid you in mastering the facts, principles and concepts discussed in your text. There are 15 chapters in the *Study Guide*, one to accompany each of the 15 chapters in your textbook. These chapters in the *Study Guide* provide various kinds of review activities which I shall describe in a moment. Collectively, these review activities should provide you with a great deal of assistance in preparing for exams.

The second part of this book is the *Personal Explorations Workbook*. This portion of the book contains two kinds of activities designed to foster personal insights. These are: (1) a series of personal probes intended to make you think about yourself in depth, and (2) a series of psychological scales which you can administer to yourself. How you use these personal exploration exercises will depend, in part, on your instructor. Some instructors will want to assign some of these personal exploration exercises and then collect them for individual scrutiny or class discussion. That is why the pages of this book are perforated -- to make it convenient for those instructors who like to assign such exercises as homework. Other instructors may not wish to assign this kind of homework. In such cases, it will be up to you to decide whether you want to make use of the personal exploration exercises. I believe that even if they are not assigned, you will find many of them to be very interesting. I strongly encourage you to look over the exercises; I am confident that you will enjoy working on many of them.

Wayne Weiten

CREDITS

Contents

PSYCHOLOGICAL SCALES

Part I
Introduction to the Study Guide

You will find your *Study Guide* in Part I of this book. You should use it to help you master the material in your textbook. You will find four kinds of review activities for each chapter. These include: (1) a review of principal ideas based on learning objectives, (2) a review of new terms or vocabulary items, (3) a review of important people, and (4) a self-test.

IDEAS: REVIEW OF LEARNING OBJECTIVES

Learning objectives are precise statements of what you should know after having mastered the assigned reading. A list of learning objectives is provided for each chapter. They follow the order of presentation in the text. Under each learning objective there is space for you to summarize the idea(s) addressed by each objective. The space isn't very large, but that's done on purpose. You need to figure out what's important and summarize it very briefly. There are limits to what you can memorize. Hopefully, the moderate amount of space will force you to be very concise in capturing the critical ideas found in your book.

TERMS: REVIEW OF NEW VOCABULARY

The discipline of psychology employs a lot of technical terms or jargon. Many of these terms will be new to many readers. Learning this terminology is one of the important elements in your educational endeavor. The running glossary and alphabetical glossary in your text are designed to help you with these new terms. This review feature in your *Study Guide* allows you to double-check your learning of this technical terminology. All of the new terms introduced in the chapter are listed in alphabetical order. Under this list you will find a series of brief definitions for terms in the order in which they appeared in the chapter. Your task is to fill in the appropriate term for each definition. This will allow you to test your learning of your new vocabulary. Moreover, once you fill in all of the blanks you will have a handy and concise list of new terms to study prior to your exam. You can easily check your answers for these exercises by referring back to the running glossary for the chapter.

PEOPLE: REVIEW OF MAJOR THEORISTS AND RESEARCHERS

Most instructors believe that it is more important to know ideas than people and I agree. However, learning about a discipline does entail learning about major contributors to the discipline. This third review feature in your *Study Guide* lists the important people discussed in each chapter. I have tried to keep these lists of people fairly short, limiting them to major contributors as discussed by your book, because I believe that there is little to be gained by an undue emphasis on names. Nonetheless, this review feature should help you to quickly identify which names you need to know. Each list of names is accompanied by a list of accomplishments, theories, and contributions which can be matched with the names. This matching task should permit you to quickly ascertain whether or not you know who's who.

SELF-TEST

The fourth feature of your *Study Guide* is a 15-item true-false test (10 items for shorter chapters) which will allow you to check your overall understanding of the material in the chapter. You should wait to take this self-test until you feel pretty confident about your mastery of the chapter. If you have, indeed, studied effectively, you should get 80 to 100 percent of the items correct. The answers can be found at the bottom of the self-test. They are listed in order, but unnumbered. The lack of numbering should prevent you from gazing downward and "cheating" easily, while at the same time, it should make scoring fairly convenient.

Chapter One Review

IDEAS: REVIEW OF LEARNING OBJECTIVES
_____

When you have mastered the material in this chapter you should be able to do the following.

1. Summarize the theme of Fromm's book <u>Escape from Freedom</u>.

2. Summarize the theme of Toffler's book <u>Future Shock</u>.

3. List four factors which appear to draw people to unorthodox religious groups (based on research by Cox).

4. Discuss some of the reasons why unorthodox religious groups generally do not provide satisfactory solutions to the search for direction.

5. List three problems that are common in popular "self-help" books.

6. Discuss the two meanings of the term <u>adjustment</u>.

7. List the assumptions upon which the scientific endeavor is based.

8. List the three sets of goals for the science of psychology.

9. Describe two major steps in a scientific investigation.

10. Describe two advantages of the scientific approach to understanding behavior.

11. List seven factors which do not appear to be crucial determinants of happiness.

12. Discuss the relationship between love and happiness.

13. Discuss the relationship between marriage and happiness.

14. Discuss the relationship between work and happiness.

TERMS: REVIEW OF NEW VOCABULARY

Fill in the appropriate term for each definition.

Adjustment   Hedonism   Personality
Behavior   Hypothesis   Psychology
Determinism   Narcissism   Reference group
Empiricism   Operational definition Subjects
Future shock

_____ 1. Disorientation due to rapid cultural change.

_____ 2. Excessive self-love.

_____ 3. Devotion to the pursuit of pleasure.

_____ 4. Scientific study of behavior.

_____ 5. Responses of an organism.

_____ 6. Process of coping with demands and pressures.

_____ 7. A person's characteristic patterns of behavior.

_____ 8. Events are governed by some lawful order.

_____ 9. Knowledge should be acquired through observation.

_____ 10. Prediction about relationship between two or
                       more variables.

_____ 11. Members of sample in research.

_____ 12.   Definition stated in terms of operations used to measure concept.

_____ 13.   Group against which you compare yourself according to social-comparison theory.

PEOPLE: REVIEW OF MAJOR THEORISTS AND RESEARCHERS

Match the people with their contributions and/or ideas.

A.   Alvin Toffler

B.   Jonathan Freedman

C.   Erich Fromm

_____ 1.   Proposed that people may find freedom aversive.

_____ 2.   Argued that rapid cultural change may promote psychological distress.

_____ 3.   Conducted extensive research on the determinants of happiness.

SELF-TEST

Answer the following questions true or false and check your responses with the answer key below.

_____ 1.   According to Fromm, there is nothing that people value and protect more than their freedom.

_____ 2.   According to Cox, joining unorthodox religious groups is an excellent way to deal with modern adjustment problems.

_____ 3.   Self-help books only rarely provide explicit directions about how to change your behavior.

_____ 4.   Psychology is interested exclusively in human behavior.

_____ 5.   Your text argues that the term adjustment should be discarded from our scientific vocabulary.

_____ 6.   Scientific research is based on the assumptions of determinism and empiricism.

_____ 7.   Measurement, description, understanding, prediction and application are all goals of the scientific method.

_____ 8.   The scientific approach to understanding behavior is no better than common sense.

_____ 9.   Freedman concludes that wealth, health and religion are major determinants of happiness.

_____ 10.   According to Freedman, evaluations of happiness are relative.

KEY: F F T F F T T F F T

Chapter Two Review

<u>IDEAS: REVIEW OF LEARNING OBJECTIVES</u>

When you have mastered the material in this chapter you should be able to do the following.

1. Explain the three functions of a theory.

2. List the three major theoretical orientations in psychology.

3. Describe the three structural components of personality proposed by Freud.

4. Describe Freud's three levels of awareness.

5.   Identify the drives that Freud thought were most significant in governing behavior.

6.   Explain the operation of Freud's conflict model of personality.

7.   List and describe the first three stages of psychosexual development proposed by Freud.

8.   Identify the innovative aspects of Erikson's theory of psychosocial development.

9.   Compare and contrast Freud's and Erikson's stage theories of development.

10.   List the major trends in Neofreudian theories of personality.

11.   List four significant contributions of psychoanalytic theory.

12.   List four shortcomings of psychoanalytic theory.

13.   Summarize behaviorists' view regarding structural constructs in personality theory.

14.   List three types of conditioning.

15.   Explain how responses are acquired through respondent conditioning.

16.   Describe the kinds of responses that tend to be governed by respondent conditioning in everyday life.

17.   Explain how responses are acquired through operant conditioning.

18.   Summarize how discriminative stimuli influence operant behavior.

19. Describe observational learning.

20. Describe the behaviorist model of motivation.

21. List four significant contributions of behavioristic theory.

22. List four shortcomings of behavioristic theory.

23. List the major principles of humanistic philosophy.

24. Describe Rogers' construct of the self-concept.

25. Summarize Rogers' views on why people develop incongruence between their self-concept and reality.

26. Describe the operation of Rogers' self-actualizing tendency.

27. Describe Maslow's hierarchy of needs and how it works.

28. List several metaneeds proposed by Maslow.

29. List four significant contributions of humanistic theory.

30. List four shortcomings of humanistic theory.

31. Compare the psychoanalytic, behavioristic and humanistic models in regard to their assumptions about human nature.

32. List the two general categories into which psychological tests fall.

33. Summarize the problems associated with personality self-report inventories.

34. Explain why psychological tests should be reliable and valid.

TERMS: REVIEW OF NEW VOCABULARY

Fill in the appropriate term for each definition.

Acquisition
Behaviorism
Cognitive
Conditioned
   response
Conditioned
   stimulus
Conditioning
Conscious
Construct
Correlation
   coefficient
Defense
   mechanism
Discrimination
Discriminative stimuli
Drive
Ego
Elicit
Emit
Extinction
Fixation
Generalization
Habit hierarchy
Holistic
Humanism

Id
Identification
Incongruence
Insight therapy
Libido
Model
Metaneeds
Negative
   reinforcement
Neo-Freudian
Norms
Observational
   learning
Oedipal
   complex
Operant
   conditioning
Paradigm
Phenomenological
Pleasure
   principle
Positive
   reinforcement
Preconscious
Primary drives
Primary
   reinforcers
Psychoanalysis

Psychoanalytic model
Psychopathic personality
Punishment
Reality principle
Reliability
Respondent conditioning
Secondary drives
Secondary reinforcers
Self-actualization
Self-actualizing
   tendency
Self-concept
Stage
Standardization
Stimulus-response bond
Superego
Trait
Theory
Unconditioned response
Unconditioned stimulus
Unconscious
Validity

_____ 1. A set of hypotheses explaining relations among a set of variables.

_____ 2. A theoretical concept used for explanatory purposes.

_____ 3. Major theoretical orientation in psychology based on the work of Freud.

_____ 4. Freudian approach to psychotherapy.

_____ 5. In psychoanalytic theory, the personality component that operates according to the pleasure principle.

_____ 6. In psychoanalytic theory, the personality component that operates according to the reality principle.

_____ 7. Emphasizes immediate gratification of instinctual urges.

_____ 8. In psychoanalytic theory, raw, instinctual, psychic energy.

_____ 9. Emphasizes social realities which may require delay of gratification.

_____ 10. In psychoanalytic theory, the personality component that houses moral codes.

_____ 11. The portion of the psyche containing material of which the ego is aware.

_____ 12. The portion of the psyche containing material just below the surface of awareness.

_____ 13. The portion of the psyche containing material that is beyond easily accessible awareness.

_____ 14. A largely cognitive coping process that attempts to ward off unpleasant emotions through distortion of reality.

_____ 15. Failure to move forward from one developmental stage to another.

_____ 16. A period in human development during which certain characteristic patterns of behavior are exhibited.

_____ 17. A child's erotic desire for opposite-sex parent coupled with hostility toward same-sex parent.

_____ 18. Perception of similarity to another. Also a defense mechanism involving the formation of an alliance with an admired person or group.

_____ 19. Personality theories that are variations on original psychoanalytic themes.

_____ 20. Major theoretical orientation that argues that only observable behavior should be studied.

_____ 21. A collection of response tendencies in order of strength.

_____ 22. Pertaining to thought.

_____ 23. The formation, strengthening and weakening of response tendencies.

_____ 24. Synonymous with classical conditioning.

_____ 25. Association between an event and an organism's reaction to the event.

_____ 26. A model or strategy for doing research.

_____ 27. Stimulus that evokes unconditioned response.

_____ 28. Natural reaction to unconditioned stimulus.

_____ 29. Stimulus that acquires capacity to elicit conditioned response.

_____ 30. Reaction evoked by conditioned stimulus.

_____ 31. The automatic evocation of a response in respondent conditioning.

_____ 32. Phase during which a new conditioned response is acquired.

_____ 33. The weakening of a tendency to make a response.

_____ 34. Tendency to respond to different stimuli with same response.

_____ 35. Tendency to respond differentially to similar stimuli.

_____ 36. Synonymous with instrumental conditioning.

_____ 37. Voluntary expression of a response in operant conditioning.

_____ 38. Strengthening of a response tendency by the delivery of a pleasant stimulus.

_____ 39. Strengthening of a response tendency by the removal of an unpleasant stimulus.

_____ 40. Presentation of a noxious stimulus.

_____ 41. Stimuli that signal the probability of reinforcement.

_____ 42. Vicarious conditioning or modeling.

_____ 43. Person whose behavior is imitated in vicarious conditioning.

_____ 44. State which activates and directs behavior.

_____ 45. Unlearned, physiological needs.

_____ 46. Learned, conditioned needs.

_____ 47. Unlearned reinforcers.

_____ 48. Conditioned reinforcers.

_____ 49. Major theoretical orientation that emphasizes unique qualities of humans.

_____ 50. Emphasis on personal, subjective view of events.

_____51. Emphasis on unified, integrated organization of behavior.

_____52. A collection of beliefs about one's own nature.

_____53. In Rogers' theory, disparity between self-concept and actual experience.

_____54. In Rogers' theory, the tendency to be consistent with one's self-concept.

_____55. Personality disorder marked by impulsive, manipulative and amoral behavior.

_____56. In Maslow's theory, the need to fulfill one's potential.

_____57. Growth needs in Maslow's hierarchy.

_____58. Treatment process emphasizing improved self-understanding.

_____59. A personality characteristic.

_____60. Uniformity in administration and scoring of a psychological test.

_____61. Information on what is a high or low score on a psychological test.

_____62. Degree to which a test measures consistently.

_____63. Degree to which a test measures what it was designed to measure.

_____64. A statistic which is an index of the kind and degree of relationship between two variables.

PEOPLE: REVIEW OF MAJOR THEORISTS AND RESEARCHERS

Match the people with their contributions and/or ideas.

A. Alfred Adler

B. Albert Bandura

C. Erik Erikson

D. Sigmund Freud

E. Carl Jung

F. Abraham Maslow

G. Ivan Pavlov

H. Carl Rogers

I. B.F. Skinner

J. John B. Watson

_____ 1. Father of psychoanalytic theory.

_____ 2. Author of neo-freudian theory emphasizing 8 stages of psycho-social development.

_____ 3. Neo-freudian theorist who stressed conscious processes, the influence of social factors, and the drive for superiority.

_____ 4. Neo-freudian theorist who de-emphasized sexuality and invented idea of collective unconscious.

_____ 5. Early and vocal advocate of behaviorism.

_____ 6. Provided first demonstration of respondent conditioning.

_____ 7. Conducted pioneering investigation of operant conditioning.

_____ 8. Described process of observational learning.

_____ 9. Humanistic theorist whose ideas center around construct of self-concept.

_____ 10. Humanistic theorist who emphasized need for self-actualization and hierarchical organization of needs.

SELF-TEST

Indicate whether the following statements are true or false and check your responses with the answer key below.

_____ 1. The three major theoretical orientations in psychology discussed in your text are structuralism, behaviorism and humanism.

_____ 2. Freud believed that the sex and aggression drives were the most significant in governing behavior.

_____ 3. The first stage in Freud's model of psychosexual development is the anal stage.

_____ 4. According to psychoanalytic theory, resolution of the Oedipal complex is crucial to healthy psychosexual development.

_____ 5. Neo-Freudian theories reduced Freud's original emphasis on the importance of sexuality and childhood experience.

_____ 6. Psychoanalytic theory has been criticized for its overly positive view of human nature.

_____ 7. The behaviorists propose the self-concept as their major personality structure.

_____ 8. Respondent conditioning was originally demonstrated by B.F. Skinner.

_____ 9. In respondent conditioning, responses are said to be emitted.

_____ 10. In operant conditioning, responses are strengthened by both positive and negative reinforcement.

_____ 11. Behaviorists have been criticized for depending too much on animal research.

_____ 12. Humanism rejects the phenomenological approach to understanding behavior.

_____ 13. Two important humanistic theorists are Carl Rogers and Abe Maslow.

_____ 14. According to Maslow, metaneeds are not really needs at all.

_____ 15. Validity is the consistency of a test's measurement.

KEY: F T F T F F F F F T T F T F F

Chapter Three Review

IDEAS: REVIEW OF LEARNING OBJECTIVES

When you have mastered the material in this chapter you should be able to do the following.

1. Discuss the relationship between physical and psychological stress.

2. Explain some implications of the fact that the perception of stress is subjective.

3. Describe the Type A personality.

4. List four principal sources of stress.

5. Describe three types of conflict and their typical effects upon behavior.

6. Describe two kinds of pressure.

7. Discuss the evidence that change is, in and of itself, stressful.

8. Describe how repressors and sensitizers react differently to stress.

9. Explain how stress severity is influenced by one's resources for coping with the stress and familiarity with the stress.

10. Explain how the imminence of stress and the duration of stress influence its severity.

11. Explain how the stress of multiple demands may have cumulative effects.

12. List three dimensions of emotion commonly elicited by stress.

13. Discuss the possible effects of emotional arousal on intellectual functioning and coping efforts.

14. Describe the three stages of Selye's General Adaption Syndrome.

15. Describe evidence on the link between stress and peptic ulcers.

16. Describe evidence on the link between stress and coronary disease.

17. Describe the relationship between frustration and aggression.

18. Discuss the adaptive value of aggression as a response to stress.

19. Describe the learned helplessness syndrome and its apparent cause.

20. Discuss the adaptive value of withdrawal as a response to stress.

21. Specify what defense mechanisms defend against, and how they work.

22. Discuss whether defense mechanisms are unconscious and normal.

23. List the nine defense mechanisms described in the text.

24. Discuss the adaptive value of defense mechanisms.

25. Describe four characteristics of constructive coping.

26. List three personality traits related to stress tolerance (based on Kobasa's research).

27. Discuss how constitutional factors may influence stress tolerance.

28. Discuss how early trauma may influence stress tolerance.

29. Describe the Social Readjustment Rating Scale (SRRS).

30. Explain why one should be cautious in interpreting the apparent link between SRRS scores and general health.

TERMS: REVIEW OF NEW VOCABULARY
_____

Fill in the appropriate term for each definition.

Adrenocorticotrophin	Conflict	Learned helplessness
Aggression	Defense mechanism	Neurotic
Approach-Approach conflict	Denial	Pituitary gland
Approach-Avoidance conflict	Displacement	Pressure
	Emotion	Projection
Autonomic nervous system	Fantasy	Psychosomatic disorders
	Frustration	Rationalization
Avoidance-Avoidance conflict	General adaption syndrome	Reaction formation
	Identification	Regression
		Repression

Repressor   Stress   Trait anxiety
Sensitizer   Stress tolerance   Type A personality
State anxiety

_____ 1. Events that tax our adaptive capacities by threatening our well-being.

_____ 2. A moderately severe form of psychopathology dominated by anxiety and defensiveness.

_____ 3. Personality syndrome marked by aggressive, competitive, time-conscious behavior.

_____ 4. The blocking of some goal pursuit.

_____ 5. Arousal of incompatible motives.

_____ 6. Choice between two attractive goals.

_____ 7. Choice between two unattractive goals.

_____ 8. Choice about a goal which is both attractive and repulsive.

_____ 9. Expectations that one behave in a certain way.

_____ 10. Personality type that avoids facing up to threat.

_____ 11. Personality type that is overly sensitive to possible threat.

_____ 12. State involving feelings which are difficult to control.

_____ 13. Temporary experience of worry and tension.

_____ 14. Personality trait involving anxiety-proneness.

_____ 15. Selye's 3-stage model of the bodily response to stress.

_____ 16. Controls glands, smooth muscles, heart and blood vessels.

_____ 17. Secretes hormones regulating growth and other glands.

_____ 18. Hormone which stimulates adrenal cortex.

_____ 19. Physical illnesses believed to be caused, in part, by psychological factors.

_____ 20. Behavior intended to hurt someone.

_____ 21. Passive behavior produced by exposure to unavoidable aversive events.

_____ 22. Coping process used to ward off unpleasant emotions through self-deception.

_____ 23. Keeping threatening thoughts unconscious.

_____ 24. Conscious refusal to accept the truth.

_____ 25. Attribution of one's own unacceptable thoughts or feelings to another.

_____26. Redirection of hostility to irrelevant recipient.

_____27. Effort to behave in manner that is opposite of one's true feelings.

_____28. Return to less mature form of behavior.

_____29. Creation of false but plausible excuses for unacceptable behavior.

_____30. Creation of real or imaginary alliance with some admired person or group in order to boost self-esteem.

_____31. Imagining the attainment of satisfactions.

_____32. Capacity to resist stress.

PEOPLE: REVIEW OF MAJOR THEORISTS AND RESEARCHERS

Match the people with their contributions and/or ideas.

A. Hans Eysenck

B. Friedman & Rosenman

C. Holmes & Rahe

D. S. Kobasa

E. Hans Selye

F. M.E.P. Seligman

G. Marvin Zuckerman

_____ 1. Described Type A personality.

_____ 2. Developed SRRS.

_____ 3. Described General Adaption Syndrome.

_____ 4. Described learned helplessness.

_____ 5. Conducted research on personality determinants of stress tolerance.

_____ 6. Theorized that ANS sensitivity may be crucial determinant of stress tolerance.

_____ 7. Described Sensation-seeking syndrome.

SELF-TEST

Indicate whether the following statements are true or false and check your responses with the answer key below.

_____ 1. Stress may be either physical or psychological.

_____ 2. Stress is always externally imposed upon a person.

_____ 3. The four principal kinds of stress are: frustration, change, pressure and loss.

_____ 4. In an avoidance-avoidance conflict, people tend to delay their decision.

_____ 5. Perceptions of stress are subjective and personal.

_____ 6. Sensitizers tend to deny the existence of threat.

_____ 7. Emotional arousal always improves task performance.

_____ 8. In the alarm stage of the General Adaption Syndrome, the parasympathetic division of the ANS goes to work.

_____ 9. Peptic ulcers are no longer believed to be stress related.

_____10. Frustration inevitably leads to aggression.

_____11. Learned helplessness is caused by the experience of uncontrollable aversive events.

_____12. Defense mechanisms are a clear sign of abnormality.

_____13. Reaction formation involves the redirection of hostility toward an irrelevant recipient.

_____14. Early psychological traumas have been related to heightened vulnerability to stress.

_____15. Caution is in order when interpreting one's SRRS scores.

KEY: T F F T T F F F F T F F T T

Chapter Four Review

IDEAS: REVIEW OF LEARNING OBJECTIVES

When you have mastered the material in this chapter you should be able to do the following.

1. List and describe 3 characteristics of psychological health as theorized by Freud.

2. Describe Jung's point of view on psychological health.

3. Describe the similar views of Adler and Fromm on psychological health.

4. Describe Erikson's view regarding the nature of psychological health.

5. Describe the view on psychological health taken by the behaviorists.

6. Describe 3 characteristics of Rogers' fully-functioning person.

7. Discuss Maslow's research on psychological health.

8. List 12 characteristics of Maslow's self-actualizing person.

9. Describe 4 characteristics of psychological health as theorized by Perls.

10. Discuss 3 problems with models of psychological health.

11. List 8 qualities representing the core of psychological health, according to your text.

12. Describe Ellis' A-B-C analysis of how thoughts cause emotions.

13. Describe 5 common patterns of irrational thought.

14. Discuss how one can change irrational thought patterns.

15. Discuss the value of trying to release pent-up emotions.

16. Describe 3 possible links between nutrition and mental health.

17. List some of the possible effects of sleep deprivation.

18. Discuss the importance of REM sleep.

19.   Summarize several potential benefits of regular exercise.

20.   List 4 guidelines for embarking on an exercise program.

21.   Discuss the value of learning to relax effectively.

22.   List 4 steps in systematic problem-solving efforts.

23.   Describe 2 tendencies which hinder people in their effort to clarify their problems.

24.   Describe 3 criteria that should be considered in evaluating alternative courses of action.

25.   List 3 procedures requiring special training that can be used to promote effective relaxation.

26. List 4 requirements to practice Benson's relaxation response.

27. Describe Benson's relaxation response procedure.

TERMS: REVIEW OF NEW VOCABULARY

Fill in the appropriate term for each definition.

Biofeedback system   Ethnocentric   REM sleep
Brainstorming   Free-floating   Sublimation
Catharsis   anxiety   Systematic
Constructive coping   Gestalt therapy   desensitization
Electroencephalograph   Hyperkinesis   Transcendental meditation

_____ 1. Redirection of libidinal energy into socially
                          acceptable activities.

_____ 2. Humanistic approach to therapy pioneered by
                          Fritz Perls.

_____ 3. Bias based on cultural background.

_____ 4. Relatively healthy efforts to deal with stress.

_____ 5. Release of emotional tension.

_____ 6. Childhood disorder marked by overactivity and
                          distractibility.

_____ 7. Stage of sleep during which rapid eye movements
                          and dreaming occur.

_____ 8. Device used to monitor electrical activity in
                          the brain.

_____ 9. Free expression of ideas while criticism is
                          withheld.

_____10. A behavior therapy used to reduce clients'
                          anxiety responses.

_____11. Worry and tension that is not associated with a
                          specific source.

_____12. Provision of information about internal bodily
                          processes in order to gain some control over
                          those processes.

_____13. A Westernized form of meditation.

PEOPLE: REVIEW OF MAJOR THEORISTS AND RESEARCHERS

Match the people with their contributions and/or ideas.

A.   Alfred Adler

B.   Herbert Benson

C.   Albert Ellis

D.   Erik Erikson

E.   Sigmund Freud

F.   Erich Fromm

G.   Carl Jung

H.   Abe Maslow

I.   Fritz Perls

J.   Carl Rogers

_____ 1.   Healthy personality marked by ego-strength, ability to work, and ability to love.

_____ 2.   Healthy personality involves balance between polarities.

_____ 3.   Healthy personality displays strong social interest.

_____ 4.   Healthy personality displays open, tolerant, trusting qualities.

_____ 5.   Healthy personality depends on outcomes of psychosocial crises.

_____ 6.   Fully functioning person is free, open and intuitive.

_____ 7.   Actually studied people of exceptional health, described self-actualizing people.

_____ 8.   Gestalt theorist, emphasized being present-oriented and free of external regulation.

_____ 9.   Emotional reactions caused by irrational thinking.

_____ 10.   Described relaxation response.

SELF-TEST

Indicate whether the following statements are true or false and check your responses with the answer key below.

_____ 1.   Freud was the first theorist to emphasize a balance between polarities as an element of psychological health.

_____ 2.   Erikson is one of the few behaviorists to take a clear position on psychological health.

_____ 3.   Rogers endorses the value of trusting one's intuitive feelings.

_____ 4.   According to Maslow, self-actualizing people are spontaneous, problem-centered and democratic.

_____ 5.   According to Maslow, self-actualizing people express their resentments openly.

_____ 6.   Models of psychological health tend to be ethnocentric.

_____ 7.   Constructive coping should be task-relevant and action-oriented.

_____ 8. According to Ellis, it is quite reasonable to expect to perform well in all endeavors.

_____ 9. Crying is clearly an unhealthy behavior.

_____ 10. Catharsis is a redirection of instinctual energy into socially acceptable activities.

_____ 11. Nutrition is entirely unrelated to mental health.

_____ 12. REM deprivation may lead to heightened irritability, anxiety and fatigue.

_____ 13. Exercise programs should move forward rapidly and involve competition.

_____ 14. Systematic desensitization was developed by Herbert Benson.

_____ 15. The relaxation response is a demystified version of meditation.

KEY: F F T T F T T F F F F T F F T

Chapter Five Review

IDEAS: REVIEW OF LEARNING OBJECTIVES
_____

When you have mastered the material in this chapter you should be able
to do the following.

1. List 3 assumptions underlying the behavioral approach to problems.

2. Explain the recipe for weight loss and describe the best way to go
    about it.

3. List the 5 steps involved in developing and executing a self-
    modification program.

4. Explain why traits cannot be a target behavior.

5. Explain the concepts of behavioral excess and deficit, and note which concept is best when you have a choice.

6. List 3 kinds of information you should pursue in gathering your baseline data.

7. Explain why it may be useful to know about the common antecedents of your target behavior.

8. Discuss some advice regarding the identification of the consequences of your target behavior.

9. Discuss how to select a reinforcer for your program.

10. Discuss how to set up reinforcement contingencies.

11. Define shaping and explain when you would use it.

12.   Describe a token economy and some of its advantages.

13.   Describe 4 strategies for decreasing the strength of an unwanted response.

14.   Describe two problems in the use of punishment and two guidelines for its usage.

15.   Discuss the value of a behavioral contract.

16.   Discuss how you should react if your program is not a success.

17.   Describe the ways in which your program may come to an end.

18.   Describe the concept of drug abuse.

19.   Distinguish between physical and psychological dependence.

20.   List the principal narcotics and describe their effects.

21.   List the risks associated with the use of narcotics.

22.   List the principal sedatives and describe their effects.

23.   List the risks associated with the use of sedatives.

24.   List the principal stimulants and describe their effects.

25.   List the risks associated with the use of stimulants.

26. List the principal hallucinogens and describe their effects.

27. List the risks associated with the use of hallucinogens.

28. List the principal cannabis derivatives and their effects.

29. List the risks associated with the use of cannabis.

30. Describe the effects of alcohol.

31. List the risks associated with the use of alcohol.

TERMS: REVIEW OF NEW VOCABULARY

Fill in the appropriate term for each definition.

Addiction	Baseline period	Contract
Adipocytes	Behavior modification	Cross tolerance
Antecedents	Behavioral deficit	Drug
Basal metabolic rate	Behavioral excess	Drug abuse
	Cannabis	Endocrine system

Extinction
Flashback
Hallucinations
Hallucinogens
Intermittent
   reinforcement
Intravenous
   injection
Narcotics
Neurotransmitter

Obesity
Overdose
Paranoia
Paranoid
   schizophrenia
Physical dependence
Psychological
   dependence
Psychosis
Punishment

Reinforcement
   contingencies
Reverse tolerance
Shaping
Sedatives
Stimulants
Token economy
Tolerance
Withdrawal syndrome

_____ 1. Approach to altering behavior that uses principles of learning.

_____ 2. Condition of being overweight.

_____ 3. Fat cells.

_____ 4. Resting energy output of the body.

_____ 5. Response that occurs too infrequently.

_____ 6. Response that occurs too frequently.

_____ 7. Period prior to behavioral intervention during which target behavior is observed.

_____ 8. Events that frequently precede the target behavior.

_____ 9. Reinforcement schedule wherein only some of the designated responses are reinforced.

_____ 10. Rules that govern the delivery of reinforcers.

_____ 11. Reinforcement of closer and closer approximations of the desired response.

_____ 12. System for doling out symbolic reinforcers.

_____ 13. Termination of reinforcement.

_____ 14. Presentation of an aversive stimulus.

_____ 15. Written agreement to follow contingencies spelled out in behavior-modification program.

_____ 16. Drug use not condoned by one's society.

_____ 17. Chemical substance that alters psychological and physiological functioning.

_____ 18. Gradual reduction in response to a drug.

_____ 19. Condition where termination of drug use leads to extreme physical distress.

_____ 20. Physical dependence.

_____ 21. Physical distress due to termination of drug use.

_____ 22. Mental and emotional dependence on a drug.

_____ 23. Excessive drug dose that could lead to death.

_____ 24. Drugs that have sedative and analgesic effects.

_____ 25. Direct injection into blood vein with hypodermic needle.

_____ 26. Drugs that have depressant and sleep-producing effects.

_____ 27. Drugs that tend to increase behavioral activity.

_____ 28. Chemical substance involved in neural transmission.

_____ 29. Feelings of being persecuted.

_____ 30. Disturbances involving severe impairment of reality contact.

_____ 31. Disorder marked by irrational thought processes, delusions of persecution and grandeur.

_____ 32. Drugs marked by their prominent hallucinatory effects.

_____ 33. Sensory distortions.

_____ 34. Tolerance to one drug produced by use of another drug.

_____ 35. Spontaneous, vivid recurrence of drug-induced experience.

_____ 36. Hemp plant from which marijuana comes.

_____ 37. Gradual increase in response to a drug.

_____ 38. Ductless glands of the body.

PEOPLE: REVIEW OF MAJOR THEORISTS AND RESEARCHERS

Match the people with their contributions and/or ideas.

A. Stanley Schachter

B. Stuart & Davis

C. Watson & Tharp

_____ 1. Spelled out techniques of self-modification.

_____ 2. Believes that excessive focus on external food cues leads to obesity.

_____ 3. Provided excellent programs to conquer obesity with behavior modification.

SELF-TEST

Indicate whether the following statements are true or false and check your responses with the answer key below.

_____ 1. Behaviorists believe that the quality of one's adjustment may vary tremendously from one situation to another.

_____ 2. When you have a choice it is best to make your target behavior a behavioral excess instead of a behavioral deficit.

_____ 3. In most cases it is okay to skip the step in behavior mod-
          ification where you gather baseline data.

_____ 4. Sometimes a response may be its own reinforcement.

_____ 5. If you want to develop a response that you're not capable of
          making you should use a token economy.

_____ 6. Rapid reinforcement is better than delayed reinforcement.

_____ 7. If you use punishment in self-modification it should be used
          alone.

_____ 8. Behavior modification programs often require adjustments or
          fine-tuning.

_____ 9. Drug abuse inevitably is a sign of pathology.

_____10. Narcotics have no potential for producing physical dependence.

_____11. Overdose is a serious danger with sedatives.

_____12. Psychoses have sometimes been attributed to the use of
          stimulants.

_____13. Hallucinogens definitely cause chromosomal damage.

_____14. Reverse tolerance is common with the use of marijuana.

_____15. Alcohol is a harmless drug.

KEY: T F F T F T F T F F T T F T F

Chapter Six Review

IDEAS: REVIEW OF LEARNING OBJECTIVES
_____

When you have mastered the material in this chapter, you should be able to do the following.

1. Describe the attribution process, including the principal dimension along which we make attributions.

2. Describe how actors and observers are different in their attributional biases.

3. Use the concept of cognitive dissonance to explain why we strive for consistency in our beliefs.

4. Explain what selectivity in social perception involves.

5. Explain Bem's notion that we may derive our attitudes from our behavior.

6. Define self-concept and explain its prescriptive nature.

7. Summarize social comparison theory and its relation to one's self-concept.

8. Describe distortive tendencies in the formation of one's self-concept.

9. Discuss how one's locus of control might affect self-perceptions.

10. Discuss how other people may shape one's self-concept.

11. Discuss how cultural guidelines may shape one's self-concept.

12. Define self-ideal and discuss how much disparity there should be between one's self-concept and self-ideal.

13. Define self-esteem and describe some problems in its investigation.

14. List five behavioral characteristics which tend to be associated with low self-esteem.

15. Discuss the determinants of self-esteem.

16. Define and give examples of public selves.

17. Describe Goffman's view of why we engage in self-presentation.

18. Describe ingratiation techniques.

19. Explain why some people are involved in a search for their authentic self.

20. List some characteristics commonly attributed to physically attractive people.

21. List some aspects of physical appearance besides attractiveness which influence our perception of others.

22. Define stereotype and list the three types of groups most commonly stereotyped.

23. Describe the fundamental attribution error.

24. Explain what implicit theories of personality involve.

25. Define primacy effects and explain how they may promote inaccuracy in person perception.

26.   Explain what is meant by motivational error in person perception.

27.   Explain the concept of defensive attribution.

28.   Define egocentrism and explain its role in producing errors in person perception.

29.   List five sources of error in person perception which commonly contribute to racial prejudice.

30.   List three common costs to the victims of racial prejudice.

31.   Discuss how prejudice is costly at the societal level.

32.   Briefly describe seven steps which are suggested for building high self-esteem.

TERMS: REVIEW OF NEW VOCABULARY
_____

Fill in the appropriate term for each definition.

Attribution	Inferiority complex	Racism
Cognitive dissonance	Ingratiation	Reference group
Defensive attribution	Locus of control	Self-concept
Egocentrism	Motivational error	Self-esteem
Epidemiological	Prejudice	Self-ideal
Fundamental	Primacy effect	Self-perception theory
attribution error	Public self	Social-comparison
Implicit theories of	Racial	theory
personality	discrimination	Stereotype

_____ 1. Inference about the cause of behavior.

_____ 2. Tension produced by contradictory cognitions.

_____ 3. Idea that we infer our attitudes and traits from observing our own behavior.

_____ 4. Collection of beliefs about your own nature.

_____ 5. Idea that we need to compare ourselves to others in order to better understand ourselves.

_____ 6. Group of people you choose to compare yourself against.

_____ 7. Personality trait involving belief about degree to which you control your fate.

_____ 8. Person's image of how she or he would like to be.

_____ 9. Person's own global evaluation of worth.

_____ 10. Image presented to others.

_____ 11. Effort to gain liking through careful self-presentations.

_____ 12. Oversimplified belief about a group of people which assumes that they are all alike.

_____ 13. Observers' pervasive bias in favor of internal attributions.

_____ 14. Assumptions about personality traits that go together.

_____ 15. Powerful first impression.

_____ 16. Inaccurate perceptions of others due to wishful thinking.

_____ 17. Attribution bias leading to victim derogation.

_____ 18. Belief that everyone behaves in a manner similar to oneself.

_____ 19. Negative attitude toward some group.

_____ 20. Behaving differently toward someone because of their race.

_____ 21. Effort to subjugate a racial group.

_____ 22. Based on study of distribution of disorders in a population.

_____ 23. Personality syndrome marked by very low self-esteem.

PEOPLE: REVIEW OF MAJOR THEORISTS AND RESEARCHERS

Match the people with their contributions and/or ideas.

A. Daryl Bem

B. Stanley Coopersmith

C. Leon Festinger

D. Erving Goffman

E. E.E. Jones

F. Harold Kelley

G. Julian Rotter

_____ 1. Architect of cognitive dissonance and social comparison theories.

_____ 2. Major attribution theorist who showed how expectations influence perceptions.

_____ 3. Developed self-perception theory.

_____ 4. Developed construct of locus of control.

_____ 5. Did research on determinants of self-esteem.

_____ 6. Sociologist who contributed research and theory on public-selves and self-presentations.

_____ 7. Described ingratiation strategies.

SELF-TEST

Indicate whether the following statements are true or false and check your responses with the answer key below.

_____ 1. Attributions involve guesswork.

_____ 2. In comparison to actors, observers favor internal attributions.

_____ 3. According to self-perception theory, our attitudes determine our behavior.

_____ 4. Distortions of self-concept generally tend to be in a positive direction.

_____ 5. People with internal locus of control believe that their fate is largely beyond their control.

_____ 6. The optimal disparity between self-ideal and self-concept is none.

_____ 7. People who are low in self-esteem frequently look for flaws in others.

_____ 8. According to Goffman, we engage in impression management because it is expected of us.

_____ 9. Ingratiation is a state of tension produced by contradictory cognitions.

_____10. There is a tendency to attribute desirable characteristics to attractive people.

_____11. Racial stereotypes are a thing of the past.

_____12. When initial information carries more weight than subsequent information we call this the fundamental attribution error.

_____13. Stereotyping, primacy effects and defensive attribution may all contribute to racial prejudice.

_____14. In attempting to build self-esteem it is important to recognize that you control your self-image.

_____15. In attempting to build self-esteem it is important to let others set your standards for you because they are more realistic.

KEY: T T F T F F T T F T F F T T F

Chapter Seven Review

IDEAS: REVIEW OF LEARNING OBJECTIVES
_____

When you have mastered the material in this chapter you should be able to do the following.

1. List the four elements in the communication process.

2. List five functions of nonverbal communication.

3. Explain five general principles of nonverbal communication.

4. Discuss what may be discerned from facial cues.

5. Describe two forms of facial deceit and discuss how such deceit may be detected.

6. List four factors which influence the amount of eye contact between people.

7. Discuss the relationship between eye contact and attraction.

8. Discuss what may be discerned from postural cues.

9. Discuss the use of hand gestures in communication.

10. Describe Hall's four distance zones.

11. Discuss how people may react to invasions of personal space.

12. Explain why variations in vocal emphasis may be important.

13. List four barriers to effective communication.

14. Describe four communication behaviors that tend to elicit defensiveness.

15. Describe five communication behaviors that tend to produce a supportive, trusting climate.

16. List four guidelines for effective speaking.

17. List four guidelines for effective listening.

18. List four reasons why we need to engage in self-disclosure.

19. Discuss the relationship between self-disclosure and psychological health.

20. Discuss sex-differences in self-disclosure.

21. Discuss to whom we are likely to disclose personal information.

22. Describe the crucial situational variable that influences self-disclosure.

23. Describe a simple guideline regarding when self-disclosure is appropriate.

24. Discuss the potential value of interpersonal conflict.

25. List and describe five personal styles of dealing with conflict.

26.   List ten guidelines for constructive conflict resolution.

TERMS: REVIEW OF NEW VOCABULARY

Fill in the appropriate term for each definition.

Channel	Interpersonal conflict	Personal space
Communication barrier	Kinesics	Proxemics
Empathy	Message	Receiver
Falsification	Modulation	Self-disclosure
Interpersonal communication	Nonverbal communication	Source
	Paralanguage	Territoriality

_____ 1.   Transmission of meaning from one person to another.

_____ 2.   Person who originates a message.

_____ 3.   Information transmitted in communication.

_____ 4.   Medium through which a message is sent.

_____ 5.   Person to whom a message is sent.

_____ 6.   Transmission of meaning through non-word symbols.

_____ 7.   Study of communication through bodily movement.

_____ 8.   Study of communication through use of personal space and distance.

_____ 9.   Study of communication through aspects of vocalization.

_____ 10. Control of facial expression to downplay emotional feeling.

_____ 11. Use of facial expression to mislead an observer about felt emotions.

_____ 12. Behavior wherein area is marked off and defended as one's own.

_____ 13. Zone of space felt to belong to a person.

_____ 14. Problem that interferes with communication.

_____ 15. Ability to understand another's frame of reference.

_____ 16. Act of revealing private information about oneself to another.

_____ 17. Interpersonal disagreement or disharmony.

53 Chapter Seven

PEOPLE: REVIEW OF MAJOR THEORISTS AND RESEARCHERS

Match the people with their contributions and/or ideas.

A. Ekman & Friesen

B. Jack Gibb

C. E.T. Hall

D. Sidney Jourard

E. Albert Mehrabian

_____ 1. Conducted research on many aspects of non-verbal communication.

_____ 2. Conducted research on facial expression in nonverbal communication.

_____ 3. Theory on personal distance zones.

_____ 4. Theory about defensiveness in communication.

_____ 5. Pioneered research and theory on self-disclosure.

SELF-TEST

Indicate whether the following statements are true or false and check your responses with the answer key below.

_____ 1. Kinesics involves the study of the communicative use of personal space and distance.

_____ 2. Paralanguage involves the study of the communicative use of bodily movements.

_____ 3. Nonverbal signals may supplement verbal transmission.

_____ 4. Nonverbal communication is multi-channeled.

_____ 5. People can send deceptive messages better with their faces than with other areas of their bodies.

_____ 6. Men tend to engage in more eye contact than women.

_____ 7. Unlike animals, people do not display territoriality.

_____ 8. Carelessness often interferes with communication.

_____ 9. Defensiveness in communication is promoted by evaluation, empathy and honesty.

_____10. A positive climate for communication is promoted by withholding judgment, equality, and provisionalism.

_____11. Effective speaking is facilitated by making verbal and nonverbal messages congruent.

_____12. Self-disclosure promotes social comparison.

_____13. Self-disclosure is generally psychologically unhealthy.

_____14. Males tend to be more self-disclosing than females.

_____15. Constructive conflict resolution is aided by attacking people's ideas instead of the people themselves.

KEY: F F T T T F F T F T T T F F T

Chapter Eight Review

IDEAS: REVIEW OF LEARNING OBJECTIVES
_____

When you have mastered the material in this chapter you should be able
to do the following.

1.   Explain why group sex-differences tell us little about individuals.

2.   List 3 cognitive abilities on which the sexes differ (and the nature
     of the difference).

3.   Explain why the often cited sex-difference in cognitive style
     appears inaccurate.

4.   Indicate whether there really are sex-differences on the personality
     dimensions of aggressiveness, influenceability, emotionality and
     passivity.

5. Summarize the evidence on alleged sex-differences in regard to 5 aspects of social orientation and skills.

6. Summarize evidence about whether men have a stronger sex drive than women.

7. Discuss three explanations for the excess of women (over men) in psychotherapy.

8. Explain the nature vs. nurture controversy and the interactionist position as they relate to the development of sex-differences.

9. Review evidence relating sex-differences to brain organization.

10. List some of the reasons why biological explanations of sex-differences appear less plausible than environmental explanations.

11. List and describe 3 processes implicated in sex role socialization.

12. List 3 sources of sex role socialization.

13. Review evidence on fear of success in women.

14. Describe 2 other common problems among women that appear to stem partially from their sex role socialization.

15. List 3 common problems among men that appear to stem partially from their sex role socialization.

16. Define sexism.

17. Describe two ways in which women are victimized by economic discrimination.

18. Explain the basis for sex roles in more primitive societies.

19. Explain why sex roles are currently in transition.

20. Describe Bem's views on androgyny.

21. Discuss the actual evidence on androgyny.

22. Define assertive behavior and contrast it with passive behavior.

23. Differentiate between assertive and aggressive behavior.

24. Explain why assertive behavior is believed to be more adaptive than
     passive or aggressive behavior.

25. Describe five steps in developing and increasing assertive
     behavior.

TERMS: REVIEW OF NEW VOCABULARY

Fill in the appropriate term for each definition.

Androgyny   Homophobia   Sex differences
Assertive behavior   Hormone   Sexism
Cerebral hemispheres   Lateralization   Sex roles
Field-dependence   Parietal lobes   Socialization
Frontal lobes   Premenstrual syndrome Stereotype
Gender   Role

_____ 1. A person's biological sex.

_____ 2. Disparities between men and women in behavior.

_____ 3. Oversimplified belief about a group of people
                     that assumes that they are all alike.

_____ 4. Cognitive style involving degree to which
                     perceptions are influenced by surrounding field.

_____ 5. Process of teaching children society's norms.

_____ 6. Area of cerebrum located toward front of skull.

_____ 7. Area of cerebrum located toward upper rear areas
                     of skull.

_____ 8. The two divisions of the cerebrum.

_____ 9. Functional specialization of the cerebral
                     hemispheres.

_____ 10. Chemical secreted by endocrine glands.

_____ 11. Menstruation-related mood shift in females.

_____ 12. Expected behavior associated with a social position.

_____ 13. Behavioral expectations based on a person's gender.

_____ 14. Strong fear and intolerance of homosexuals.

_____ 15. Discrimination based on a person's sex.

_____ 16. Personality pattern involving coexistence of
                     masculine and feminine qualities.

_____ 17. Standing up for one's rights.

PEOPLE: REVIEW OF MAJOR THEORISTS AND RESEARCHERS

Match the people with their contributions and/or ideas.

A. Sandra Bem   _____ 1. Conducted review of massive
                                      research on sex differences.
B. Phyllis Chesler
                          _____ 2. Argues that labeling bias accounts
C. Matina Horner   for excess of women in psychotherapy.

D. Maccoby & Jacklin

_____ 3. Did pioneering research on fear of success in women.

_____ 4. Theorizes that androgyny may be psychologically healthy.

SELF-TEST

Indicate whether the following statements are true or false and check your responses with the answer key below.

_____ 1. Data on sex differences allow us to make accurate predictions about individuals.

_____ 2. Males score better than females in mathematics.

_____ 3. Females are more conforming and persuasible than males.

_____ 4. Men are more love-oriented than women.

_____ 5. Women seem to be more sensitive to nonverbal cues than men.

_____ 6. Men show up in psychotherapy more frequently than women.

_____ 7. Evidence suggests that men have stronger cerebral lateralization than do women.

_____ 8. The preponderance of evidence suggests that sex differences are largely acquired through learning.

_____ 9. Sex-role socialization is promoted by differential reinforcement and self-socialization.

_____10. Sex-role socialization does not take place in schools.

_____11. A major sex-role cost for women is their inability to express emotions.

_____12. Women's fear of success appears to be due primarily to apprehension about social rejection.

_____13. The transitional period regarding sex-roles should be coming to an end very soon.

_____14. Females who score high on masculinity and low on femininity are said to be androgynous.

_____15. Assertiveness is just another name for aggressive behavior.

KEY: F T F T T F T T T F F T F F F

Chapter Nine Review

IDEAS: REVIEW OF LEARNING OBJECTIVES

When you have mastered the material in this chapter you should be able to do the following.

1. Describe Schachter's research on the relationship between stress and affiliation.

2. Describe the relationship between social support and the effects of stress.

3. Discuss how individual differences in affiliation drive might affect patterns of adjustment.

4. Discuss how physical beauty affects interpersonal attraction.

5. Explain the matching hypothesis.

6. Discuss some reasons why physical attractiveness is so important in interpersonal relationships.

7. List some characteristics of others, besides physical beauty, which tend to influence a person's attraction to them.

8. List the "interaction factors" that influence interpersonal attraction.

9. Discuss how and why proximity facilitates attraction.

10. Discuss how and why similarity affects attraction.

11. Summarize evidence on the complementary needs hypothesis.

12. Explain the reciprocity effect and discuss some of the limitations of this principle.

13. Explain how Bem's self-perception theory relates to the findings of Dutton and Aron.

14. Explain how social-exchange theory views the role of self-esteem in interpersonal attraction.

15. List the 5 most important ingredients of friendship according to the Parlee et al. survey.

16. Describe the stages of friendship formation proposed by Levinger.

17. Discuss how marital status and sex affect patterns of friendship.

18. List 4 myths about love.

19. List the six factors which, according to Jourard, enhance the capacity for love.

20. Describe the two types of love proposed by Maslow.

21. Summarize how men and women differ in their approach to love.

22. Describe three types of loneliness.

23. Summarize evidence on the prevalence of loneliness.

24. Describe evidence on the personal consequences of loneliness.

25. List three social trends which contribute to increasing loneliness in our society.

26. List five personal factors which tend to be associated with loneliness.

27. Explain the key to coping successfully with loneliness.

28. Describe the symptoms of shyness.

29. Discuss the prevalence of shyness.

30. List 3 steps suggested by Zimbardo for coping with shyness.

31. Discuss some of Zimbardo's suggestions for improvement of social skills.

TERMS: REVIEW OF NEW VOCABULARY

Fill in the appropriate term for each definition.

Affiliation   Homogamy   Loneliness
Complementary needs   Ingratiation   Matching
Halo effect   Interpersonal attraction   hypothesis

Proximity   Shyness   Thematic Apperception Test
Reciprocity   Social-exchange theory

_____ 1. Human need to associate with other people.

_____ 2. Projective test requiring responses to ambiguous pictures.

_____ 3. Tendency to evaluate another person positively.

_____ 4. Notion that people of equal physical attractiveness will select each other for dating.

_____ 5. Rating of one characteristic influences ratings of others.

_____ 6. Tendency for people who live near each other to be attracted to each other.

_____ 7. Tendency for people who are similar to marry each other.

_____ 8. "Opposites attract" idea applied to interpersonal attraction.

_____ 9. Tendency to like people who like us.

_____ 10. Self-presentation strategy intended to gain liking.

_____ 11. View that interpersonal interactions are governed by rewards and costs.

_____ 12. Unpleasant emotion due to deficits in intimate relations with others.

_____ 13. Excessive caution in interpersonal interactions.

PEOPLE: REVIEW OF MAJOR THEORISTS AND RESEARCHERS

Match the people with their contributions and/or ideas.

A. Daryl Bem

B. Berscheid & Walster (Hatfield)

C. Donn Byrne

D. Sidney Jourard

E. George Levinger

F. Abe Maslow

G. Henry Murray

H. Zick Rubin

I. Stanley Schachter

J. Philip Zimbardo

_____ 1. Research team that has done a great deal of work on many aspects of attraction, awarded "golden fleece."

_____ 2. Researched link between stress and affiliation.

_____ 3. Assembled well-known taxonomy of needs.

_____ 4. Researched role of similarity in attraction.

_____ 5. Researched many aspects of attraction, author of Liking and Loving.

_____ 6. Author of self-perception theory.

_____ 7. Theorized about stages in development of friendship.

_____ 8. Theorized about qualities which promote a good capacity for love.

_____ 9. Differentiated between "being-love," and "deficiency love."

_____ 10. Did pioneering work on shyness.

SELF-TEST

Indicate whether the following statements are true or false and check your responses with the answer key below.

_____ 1. Schachter found that stress reduces the need to affiliate.

_____ 2. Social support may reduce the negative impact of stress.

_____ 3. Physical attractiveness influences dating behaviors but not same-sex friendships.

_____ 4. Competence may have either a positive or negative effect on one's social attractiveness.

_____ 5. People who are similar to each other are unlikely to be attracted to each other.

_____ 6. There is a wealth of empirical data which supports the complementary needs hypothesis.

_____ 7. "Playing hard to get" is the one exception to the reciprocity principle in attraction.

_____ 8. Research by Dutton and Aron (1974) provides support for the social-exchange theory of attraction.

_____ 9. Love is a purely positive experience.

_____ 10. Self-love undermines one's capacity to give love to others.

_____ 11. Women appear to be more romantic than men.

_____ 12. Fortunately, loneliness has been found to be unrelated to depression.

_____ 13. Fear of intimacy promotes loneliness in some people.

_____ 14. Zimbardo's research suggests that only about 15% of the population has ever had any problem with shyness.

_____ 15. Zimbardo's research suggests that most people who are shy are shy only in certain situations.

KEY: F T F T F F F F F F F F T F T

Chapter Ten Review

IDEAS: REVIEW OF LEARNING OBJECTIVES

When you have mastered the material in this chapter, you should be able to do the following.

1. List 5 social trends that are undermining the traditional model of marriage.

2. Discuss several poor motivations for marriage.

3. Explain how endogamy, homogamy and ideals affect mate selection.

4. Describe Murstein's stimulus-value-role theory.

5. Discuss how unrealistic expectations might affect marital adjustment.

6. Explain who benefits from traditional marital roles.

7. Discuss how gaps in role expectations may lead to marital problems.

8. Summarize the evidence on the relationship between occupational and marital satisfaction.

9. Describe the potential impact of poverty on a marriage.

10. Describe the relationship between the presence of children and marital satisfaction.

11. Discuss how frequent communication problems are in troubled marriages.

12. Discuss recent trends regarding in-law conflicts.

13. Discuss how sexual dysfunction is related to marital adjustment.

14. Discuss who tends to get jealous and how such jealousy may affect a relationship.

15. Describe how marital adjustment is affected by mutual leisure activities.

16. Discuss factors which influence the "success" of marriage counseling.

17. Summarize current estimates regarding the divorce rate.

18. Summarize evidence on the pre-divorce and post-divorce adjustment of former spouses and their children.

19.   List 4 sets of problems associated with divorce.

20.   List 4 post-divorce syndromes to be avoided.

21.   Summarize the data on remarriage.

22.   Describe evidence on the prevalence of cohabitation and discuss whether it is a serious threat to marriage.

23.   Describe the fundamental principles of open marriage.

24.   Discuss the value of a marriage contract.

25.   Describe two inaccurate stereotypes of single life.

26. Discuss the adjustment and happiness of single as opposed to married people.

27. Describe 3 myths regarding homosexual relationships.

28. List and describe the 5 types of homosexuals delineated by Bell and Weinberg.

29. Discuss how games may lead to problems in intimate relationships.

30. Describe the 3 ego states outlined by Berne.

31. Describe 3 types of transactions outlined by Berne.

32. Briefly describe the themes in: if it weren't for you, courtroom and corner.

33. Briefly describe the themes in: threadbare, why don't you-yes but, and sweetheart.

TERMS: REVIEW OF NEW VOCABULARY

Fill in the appropriate term for each definition.

Complementary
   transaction
Cohabitation
Crossed transaction
Ego state
Endogamy
Game
Gay

Group marriage
Heterosexual
Homogamy
Homosexual
Jealousy
Marriage
Marriage contract
Marriage counseling

Open marriage
Serial monogamy
Sexual dysfunction
Swinging
Transaction
Transactional analysis
Ulterior transaction

_____ 1. Socially sanctioned union of sexually cohabiting adults.

_____ 2. Tendency to marry within one's own social unit.

_____ 3. Tendency of similar people to marry.

_____ 4. Impairment of sexual functioning.

_____ 5. Emotional reaction to threat of losing another's affection.

_____ 6. Professional help for marital problems.

_____ 7. Sharing of a household by two unmarried, sexually cohabiting adults.

_____ 8. Marital arrangement endorsing relatively independent life-styles.

_____ 9. Written agreement spelling out marital obligations.

_____ 10. Marital arrangement based on the expectation that one will progress through a series of marriages.

_____ 11. Marital arrangement involving three or more adults.

_____ 12. Sexual relations between a married couple and at least one other person.

_____ 13. Preference for erotic activity with members of the opposite sex.

_____ 14. Non-derogatory term for homosexuals.

_____ 15. Preference for erotic activity with members of one's own sex.

_____16. Eric Berne's theory of interpersonal relations.

_____17. In transactional analysis, personality structure consisting of systems of feelings.

_____18. In transactional analysis, the fundamental unit of interaction.

_____19. Two persons communicate from compatible ego states.

_____20. Two persons communicate from incompatible ego states.

_____21. Transaction involving hidden message.

_____22. In transactional analysis, a series of manipulative interactions leading to a predictable outcome.

PEOPLE: REVIEW OF MAJOR THEORISTS

Match the people with their contributions and/or ideas.

A. Bell & Weinberg

B. Eric Berne

C. Bernard Murstein

D. O'Neill & O'Neill

_____ 1. Developed stimulus-value-role theory of mate selection.

_____ 2. Proponents of open marriage.

_____ 3. Conducted extensive research on gay relationships.

_____ 4. Architect of transactional analysis.

SELF-TEST

Indicate whether the following statements are true or false and check your responses with the answer key below.

_____ 1. In general, people are remaining single until later ages.

_____ 2. Homogamy refers to the tendency for similar people to marry.

_____ 3. According to Murstein's model, the third stage in mate-selection centers on value compatibility.

_____ 4. Unmarried men report themselves to be happier than married men.

_____ 5. Males' occupational success is positively related to their marital adjustment.

_____ 6. Childless couples report lower levels of marital satisfaction than couples with children.

_____ 7. In-law problems are the most common difficulty reported by distressed married couples.

_____ 8. Joint participation by spouses is positively related to the success of marriage counseling.

_____ 9. It is better for the children if unhappy parents remain married instead of getting a divorce.

_____10.   Statistically, second marriages are somewhat less successful than first marriages.

_____11.   Cohabitation is increasing in prevalence.

_____12.   Open marriage is the same as swinging.

_____13.   Gay couples' role expectations appear to be more flexible than heterosexuals'.

_____14.   According to Berne, ulterior transactions provide the basis for most games.

_____15.   Complementary transactions are marked by cooperation in the communication effort.

KEY: T T F F T F F T F T T F T T T

Chapter Eleven Review

When you have mastered the material in this chapter you should be able to do the following.

1. Describe three problems in doing research on sexual behavior.

2. Briefly describe the four phases in the human sexual response cycle.

3. Discuss three reasons why women tend to reach orgasm less frequently than men in coitus.

4. Describe sex differences in regard to the post-orgasm refractory period and multiple orgasms.

5. Discuss the role of fantasy in sexual arousal.

6. Discuss attitudes about self-stimulation.

7. Summarize data on the prevalence of self-stimulation.

8. Explain why foreplay is a source of discord for some couples.

9. Discuss the importance of positions and penile size in coitus.

10. Summarize data on the prevalence of oral and anal sex.

11. Explain why oral-genital sex is a source of discord for some couples.

12. Evaluate the concept of "the sexual revolution."

13. Summarize data on the prevalence of premarital sex.

14. Describe four attitudes towards premarital sex.

15. Discuss the link between marital and sexual satisfaction.

16. List some changes in marital sexual practices since the Kinsey studies.

17. Explain the impact of age on marital sexual activity.

18. Describe three types of extramarital sexual relationships.

19.   Summarize data on the prevalence of extramarital sex.

20.   List four common motivations for extramarital sex.

21.   Describe primary and secondary erectile difficulties.

22.   Discuss the causes of erectile difficulties in men.

23.   Explain why it is difficult to define premature ejaculation.

24.   Discuss the causes of premature ejaculation.

25.   Describe retarded ejaculation and spectatoring.

26. Describe primary and secondary orgasmic difficulties.

27. Discuss the causes of orgasmic difficulties in women.

28. Discuss the nature and causes of inhibited sexual desire.

29. Discuss the causes of vaginismus and dyspareunia.

30. List six general suggestions for improving sexual functioning.

31. Describe sensate focus exercises.

32. Describe strategies for coping with erectile difficulties.

33. Describe strategies for overcoming problems with premature ejaculation.

34. Describe strategies for overcoming female orgasmic difficulties.

TERMS: REVIEW OF NEW VOCABULARY

Fill in the appropriate term for each definition.

Anal sex	Erogenous zone	Retarded ejaculation
Autoeroticism	Fellatio	Sensate focus
Coitus	Foreplay	Sex therapy
Cunnilingus	Inhibited sexual desire	Sexual dysfunction
Dyspareunia	Intromission	Spectatoring
Ejaculation	Orgasm	Squeeze technique
Erectile	Orgasmic difficulties	Vaginismus
difficulties	Premature ejaculation	Vasocongestion
	Refractory period	

_____ 1. Engorgement of blood vessels.

_____ 2. Peak phase of the sexual response cycle.

_____ 3. Expulsion of semen from the penis.

_____ 4. Post-orgasmic period when males are relatively unresponsive.

_____ 5. Sexual intercourse.

_____ 6. Body area that is especially responsive to sexual stimulation.

_____ 7. Self-stimulation.

_____ 8. Sexual activities that precede intercourse.

_____ 9. Insertion of the penis into the vagina.

_____ 10. Oral stimulation of the female genitals.

_____ 11. Oral stimulation of the male genitals.

_____ 12. Penile insertion into the anus and rectum.

_____ 13. Impairment in sexual functioning.

_____ 14. Impotence.

_____ 15. Ejaculatory response that is judged to be too rapid.

_____ 16. Problems in achieving orgasm in males.

_____ 17. Excessive self-observation and detachment in sexual encounters.

_____ 18. Problems in achieving orgasm in females.

_____ 19. Lack of interest in sex.

_____ 20. Vaginal contraction that makes penile insertion painful and difficult.

_____ 21. Genital pain produced by intercourse.

_____ 22. Professional treatment of sexual problems.

_____ 23. Sex-therapy procedure wherein partners take turns pleasuring each other.

_____ 24. Sex-therapy procedure for developing better ejaculatory self-control.

PEOPLE: REVIEW OF MAJOR THEORISTS AND RESEARCHERS

Match the people with their contributions and/or ideas.

A. Morton Hunt

B. Helen S. Kaplan

C. Kinsey & associates

D. Masters & Johnson

E. Ira Reiss

_____ 1. Author of report on major survey of sexual practices published in 1974.

_____ 2. Research team that investigated sexual response cycle and developed modern sex-therapy procedures.

_____ 3. Research team that did first significant surveys on sexual practices in the late 1940s and early 1950s.

_____ 4. Investigated attitudes about premarital sex.

_____ 5. Well-known sex therapist who provided description of inhibited sexual desire.

SELF-TEST

Indicate whether the following statements are true or false and check your responses with the answer key below.

_____ 1. Unreliability in self-report is a major problem which plagues research on sexual behavior.

_____ 2. The subjective experience of orgasm in men and women is very different.

_____ 3. There is reason to believe that coitus may not provide optimal stimulation for many women.

_____ 4. Only males have a refractory period.

_____ 5. More females than males practice self-stimulation.

_____ 6. The importance of foreplay is often underestimated.

_____ 7. Fellatio is oral stimulation of the female genitals.

_____ 8. The most common viewpoint on premarital sex (according to Reiss) is permissiveness with affection.

_____ 9. It is probably best to view sexual problems as belonging to individuals rather than couples.

_____10. Hormonal imbalances are the most common cause of erectile difficulties.

_____11. A woman with primary orgasmic difficulties has never experienced an orgasm.

_____12. Inhibited sexual desire appears to be more common in women than in men.

_____13. Fantasy during sexual encounters is abnormal and dysfunctional.

_____14. The squeeze technique is used to work with erectile difficulties.

_____15. It is sometimes suggested that non-orgasmic women attempt to achieve their initial orgasms through non-coital techniques.

KEY: T F T T F T F T F F T T F F T

Chapter Twelve Review

IDEAS: REVIEW OF LEARNING OBJECTIVES

When you have mastered the material in this chapter you should be able to do the following.

1. Discuss the value of college in terms of economic benefits and job preparation.

2. Evaluate the importance of attending a prestigious college at the undergraduate level.

3. List three steps for developing sound study habits.

4. Describe the SQ3R method of reading.

5. Briefly list six tips for getting more out of lectures.

6. Specify how retention of verbal material is influenced by repetition, distributed practice, organization and meaningfulness.

7. Describe several mnemonic devices.

8. Describe six important trends affecting the work world and its future.

9. List eight general principles regarding the vocational choice process.

10. Describe six stages of vocational development.

11. List the personal characteristics that one should consider in making vocational decisions.

12. Discuss the value of occupational interest inventories as they relate to vocational choice.

13. Describe a common problem with occupational literature.

14. List eight job or occupational characteristics that one should be concerned about in vocational decisions.

15. Explain why job satisfaction may be so important to one's adjustment.

16. List nine common ingredients that contribute to job satisfaction.

17. List six principles of efficient time use on tests.

18. List five principles intended to reduce gross errors on tests.

19. List four principles for good guessing on tests.

20. List six principles of sound reasoning on tests.

21. List five principles for the utilization of secondary cues on tests.

22. List four principles for maximizing performance on essay exams.

TERMS: REVIEW OF NEW VOCABULARY
_____

Fill in the appropriate term for each definition.

Acrostic	Mnemonic device	Test-wiseness
Job satisfaction	Overlearning	Underemployment
Loci system	Retention	

_____ 1. Continued practice after apparent mastery.

_____ 2. The amount of material remembered.

_____ 3. Aid to memory which relates new material to something familiar.

_____ 4. Mnemonic device employing first letter of each word in a phrase or sentence.

_____ 5. Mnemonic device wherein images are associated with locations.

_____ 6. Job where one's talents are under utilized.

_____ 7. One's contentment with an occupation.

_____ 8. Ability to perform skillfully on exams.

PEOPLE: REVIEW OF MAJOR THEORISTS AND RESEARCHERS

Match the people with their ideas and/or contributions.

A. Caroline Bird

B. Hermann Ebbinghaus

C. Ginzberg & Super

D. F.P. Robinson

_____ 1. Proposed that college education has little financial value.

_____ 2. Developed SQ3R technique.

_____ 3. Early investigator of memory.

_____ 4. Independent theorists who described stages in vocational choice.

SELF-TEST

Indicate whether the following statements are true or false and check your responses with the answer key below.

_____ 1. Graduating from college is a major determinant of economic success.

_____ 2. In order to pursue economic success, it is critical that one go to a prestigious school.

_____ 3. Most people find studying to be a very pleasant activity.

_____ 4. Overlearning is a waste of time with little or no payoff.

_____ 5. Distributed practice promotes better retention than massed practice.

_____ 6. Underemployment should be virtually nonexistent in a few years.

_____ 7. Chance may play a role in vocational development.

_____ 8. The order of stages in vocational development is: fantasy, tentative, realistic.

_____ 9. Occupational interest inventories are excellent predictors of job success.

_____ 10. Job satisfaction is unrelated to happiness.

_____ 11. Much job dissatisfaction may come from a lack of challenge in one's work.

_____ 12. Job security is an important determinant of job satisfaction.

_____ 13. Role clarity is unrelated to job satisfaction.

_____ 14. Test-wiseness is no substitute for knowledge of the subject matter.

_____ 15. The empirical evidence consistently indicates that changing answers on tests pays off in the long run.

KEY: T F F F T F T T F F T T F T T

Chapter Thirteen Review

IDEAS: REVIEW OF LEARNING OBJECTIVES
_____

When you have mastered the material in this chapter you should be able to do the following.

1. List four criteria of psychological disorders.

2. Explain the meaning of the "medical model" of psychological disorders.

3. Summarize critics' views on the medical model.

4. List four "myths" about psychological disorders.

5. Discuss the prevalence of psychological disorders.

6. Explain three problems that are associated with psychodiagnosis and classification of mental disorders.

7. Explain the potential value of psychodiagnosis.

8. Describe generalized anxiety disorders, phobic disorders and obsessive-compulsive disorders.

9. Explain how physiological factors may be related to the etiology of anxiety disorders.

10. Explain how psychological factors may be related to the development of anxiety disorders.

11. Describe hypochondria and conversion disorders.

12. List the physiological and psychological factors that appear to be related to the etiology of somatoform disorders.

13. Describe the syndromes of amnesia, fugue and multiple-personality.

14. Describe two factors thought to be involved in the etiology of dissociative disorders.

15. Describe the two major mood disorders: depression and the bipolar affective disorder.

16. Explain how physiological factors may be related to the development of mood disorders.

17. Summarize how psychological factors may be related to the etiology of mood disorders.

18. List the general characteristics of schizophrenic disorders.

19. Describe the paranoid and catatonic subtypes of schizophrenia.

20. Describe the disorganized and undifferentiated subtypes of schizo-
     phrenia and schizoaffective disorders.

21. Describe three physiological factors that have been related to the
     etiology of schizophrenic disorders.

22. Explain how family dynamics may be related to the development of
     schizophrenic disorders.

23. Describe three other psychological considerations that may be
     involved in the etiology of schizophrenic disorders.

24. Describe paranoid disorders.

25. Discuss the etiology of paranoid disorders.

26. Describe the general nature of personality disorders.

27. Describe the psychopathic personality disorder.

28. Discuss the etiology of psychopathic personality disorders.

29. List three criteria of substance use disorders.

30. Describe evidence relating physiological factors to some substance use disorders.

31. Summarize how psychological factors may be related to the etiology of substance use disorders.

32. Summarize how age, sex and marital status are related to the incidence of suicide.

33. List five myths about suicide.

34. List six factors that can aid you in evaluating a person's suicide potential.

35. List five steps that may help to prevent someone from attempting suicide.

TERMS: REVIEW OF NEW VOCABULARY

Fill in the appropriate term for each definition.

Affective disorders	Fugue	Paranoia
Agoraphobia	Generalized anxiety	Paranoid disorders
Amnesia	disorder	Personality disorders
Antisocial personality	Hallucinations	Phobic disorder
disorder	Hypochondria	Psychodiagnosis
Anxiety disorders	Lethality	Psychopathic personality
Bipolar mood disorders	Malingering	disorder
Concordance	Manic-depressive	Psychosis
Conversion disorder	psychosis	Schizophrenic disorders
Delusion	Mood disorders	Secondary gains
Depressive disorder	Multiple-personality	Somatoform disorders
Dissociative disorders	Neurosis	Substance use disorders
Etiology	Obsessive-compulsive	Transvestitism
	disorder	

_____ 1. Condition where person achieves sexual arousal by dressing in opposite sex clothing.

_____ 2. Fear of being in open or public places.

_____ 3. DSM-II set of disorders marked by anxiety and defensive coping.

_____ 4. Classification of psychological disorders.

_____ 5. Developmental history of a disorder.

_____ 6. Class of disorders including phobic, obsessive-compulsive and generalized anxiety disorders.

_____ 7. Anxiety disorder marked by chronic high level of non-specific tension and apprehension.

_____ 8. Disorder where persistent, irrational fears of specific objects or situations dominate.

_____ 9. Disorder marked by intrusions of unwanted thoughts and urges to engage in certain actions.

_____ 10. Class of disorders including hypochondria and conversion disorders.

_____ 11. Intentional faking of an illness.

_____ 12. Disorder marked by excessive worry about the possibility of developing physical illnesses.

_____ 13. Disorder wherein person manifests physical problem for which no organic basis can be found.

_____ 14. Benefits derived from adopting sick role.

_____ 15. Class of disorders including amnesia, fugue and multiple personality.

_____ 16. Pathological loss of memory.

_____ 17. Amnesia plus flight from the scene of stress.

_____ 18. Disorder in which person manifests two or more different personalities.

_____ 19. Synonymous with mood disorders.

_____ 20. Class of disorders including depression and bipolar mood disorders.

_____ 21. DSM-II term for disorder involving manic and/or depressive episodes.

_____ 22. Disorder wherein feelings of sadness, dejection and despair dominate.

_____ 23. A belief that is out of contact with reality.

_____ 24. A sensory distortion.

_____ 25. Disorder characterized by the experience of manic and depressive states.

_____ 26. Condition that exists when both twins display the same disorder.

_____ 27. Class of disorders dominated by irrational thought processes and poor reality contact.

_____ 28. General term referring to any disturbance which significantly impairs reality contact.

_____ 29. Feelings of being persecuted.

_____ 30. Disorders marked by paranoia without personality disintegration seen in paranoid schizophrenia.

_____ 31. Class of disorders marked by extreme, maladaptive personality trait.

_____ 32. Disorder marked by impulsive, manipulative amoral behavior.

_____ 33. Synonymous with psychopathic personality disorder.

_____ 34. Pathological patterns of drug use.

_____ 35. Seriousness of one's suicide potential.

PEOPLE: REVIEW OF MAJOR THEORISTS AND RESEARCHERS

Match the people with their contributions and/or ideas.

A. Edwin Sheidman

B. Thomas Szasz

_____ 1. Critic of medical model, author of Myth of Mental Illness.

_____ 2. Conducted great deal of research on suicide.

SELF-TEST

Indicate whether the following statements are true or false and check your responses with the answer key below.

_____ 1. The four criteria of psychological disorders are: social deviance, personal distress, mood dysfunction and irrationality.

_____ 2. A strength of the medical model is that it encourages people to adopt the passive role of patient.

_____ 3. People with psychological disorders are very bizarre and very different.

_____ 4. Fortunately, reliability has never been a problem in psycho-diagnosis.

_____ 5. Agoraphobia is a somatoform disorder.

_____ 6. Mowrer proposed that anxieties are acquired through operant conditioning and maintained through respondent conditioning.

_____ 7. The dissociative disorders include amnesia, fugue and hypochondria.

_____ 8. The coexistence of two or more largely complete and usually different personalities is called schizophrenia.

_____ 9. Genetic factors do not appear to play a role in mood disorders.

_____ 10. Learned helplessness has been proposed as a model to account for schizophrenia.

_____ 11. Catatonic schizophrenia is dominated by delusions of persecution and grandeur.

_____ 12. For some inexplicable reason, people with schizophrenic disorders tend to come from exceptionally healthy homes.

_____13. Concordance rates for schizophrenia are higher for fraternal twins than they are for identical twins.

_____14. Drug problems are always a symptom of a more deeply rooted psychological disorder.

_____15. People who talk about suicide don't actually commit suicide.

KEY: F F F F F F F F F F F F F F F

Chapter Fourteen Review

IDEAS: REVIEW OF LEARNING OBJECTIVES
_____

When you have mastered the material in this chapter you should be able to do the following.

1. List the 5 general approaches to psychotherapy covered in the chapter.

2. Describe the sequence of events that leads a client into therapy.

3. Briefly describe the 4 professions which provide psychotherapy.

4. Describe the view of classical psychoanalysis on the origins of neurosis and discuss the probing of the unconscious.

5. Explain the psychoanalytic concepts of resistance, transference and interpretation.

6. List 6 trends in modified approaches to psychoanalysis.

7. Discuss the origins of psychological problems and the goals of therapy as viewed by the client-centered therapist.

8. Describe the 3 aspects of therapeutic climate believed to be important by Rogers.

9. Describe therapeutic process in client-centered therapy.

10. Summarize the principles and techniques employed by Gestalt therapy.

11. List the six general principles which form the basis for behavior therapy.

12. Describe the three phases of systematic desensitization and discuss its effectiveness.

13. Describe the purpose and nature of aversion therapy.

14. Describe the nature and uses of token economies.

15. Describe cognitive restructuring.

16. Distinguish between group therapy and encounter groups.

17. Describe the process of group therapy.

18. List 4 advantages of group therapy.

19. List the 3 general kinds of drugs used for psychotherapeutic purposes.

20. Discuss the problems associated with drug therapies.

21. Describe ECT and discuss its therapeutic effects.

22. Discuss the risks associated with ECT.

23. Summarize information on when a person should seek psychotherapy.

24. List the 5 settings in which professional therapy can be found.

25. Discuss how important a therapist's professional training, school of thought, or sex might be.

26. Summarize information on what one should look for in a prospective therapist.

27. Discuss what one should think about when dissatisfied with professional therapy.

TERMS: REVIEW OF NEW VOCABULARY

Fill in the appropriate term for each definition

Aversion therapy
Behavior therapy
Clarification
Client-centered
  therapy
Cognitive restructuring
Dream analysis

Electroconvulsive
  therapy
Encounter group
Free association
Gestalt therapy
Group therapy
Incongruence
Insight therapy

Psychoanalysis
Psychodrama
Psychotherapy
Resistance
Systematic desensitization
Tardive dyskinesia
Token economy
Transference

_____ 1. Treatment of psychological problems and disorders.

_____ 2. Approach to therapy which emphasizes probing the unconscious.

_____ 3. Psychoanalytic technique involving free expression of thoughts to probe unconscious.

_____ 4. Interpretation of symbolic content of dreams.

_____ 5. Unconscious defensiveness on the part of the client in therapy.

_____ 6. Psychoanalytic process wherein clients start relating to their therapist in ways which mimic important relationships.

_____ 7. Any verbal theory that primarily strives for enhanced self-understanding.

_____ 8. Non-directive approach to therapy which emphasizes therapeutic climate.

_____ 9. Rogers' term for disparity between self-concept and experience.

_____10. Effort to help client see problems more clearly.

_____11. Fritz Perls' approach to therapy.

_____12. Approaches to therapy based on principles of learning.

_____13. Behavior therapy designed to reduce anxiety responses.

_____14. Behavior therapy designed to eliminate undesirable responses through use of noxious stimuli.

_____15. Behavior therapy employing system for doling out symbolic reinforcers.

_____16. Behavior therapy that tries to change clients' modes of thinking.

_____17. Treatment of psychological disorders conducted with a group of people.

_____18. Psychoanalytic group therapy emphasizing role-playing.

_____19. Group experience designed to promote personal growth.

_____20. Neurological disorder produced by anti-psychotic drugs.

_____21. Therapy which triggers convulsions through electric shock.

PEOPLE: REVIEW OF MAJOR THEORISTS

Match the people with their contributions and/or ideas.

A. Sigmund Freud   ____ 1. Creator of psychoanalysis.

B. Jacob Moreno   ____ 2. Creator of client-centered therapy.

C. Fritz Perls   ____ 3. Creator of Gestalt therapy.

D. Carl Rogers   ____ 4. Creator of systematic desensitization.

E. Joseph Wolpe   ____ 5. Creator of psychodrama.

F. Irwin Yalom   ____ 6. Investigated effects of group therapy.

SELF-TEST

Indicate whether the following statements are true or false and check your responses with the answer key below.

____ 1. Many people do not seek therapy that they need because they see it as an admission of personal weakness.

____ 2. Psychologists receive an M.D. degree.

____ 3. Clients who avoid talking about sensitive issues are manifesting transference.

_____ 4. In psychoanalysis interpretations should proceed quickly and deeply.

_____ 5. Modified psychoanalytic approaches to therapy have increased emphasis on childhood and probing the unconscious.

_____ 6. In client-centered therapy climate is more important than process.

_____ 7. Gestalt therapists often work with groups.

_____ 8. Systematic desensitization looks good on paper but there is little evidence to support its efficacy.

_____ 9. Aversion therapy and the token economy are physiological approaches to treatment.

_____10. Group therapy helps participants to realize that their misery is not unique.

_____11. The three major kinds of drugs used for psychological problems are: anti-anxiety drugs, anti-psychotic drugs and anti-depressant drugs.

_____12. Tardive dyskinesia is an important new behavior therapy.

_____13. Fortunately, ECT is a risk-free procedure.

_____14. Psychotherapy can sometimes have damaging effects on clients.

_____15. A therapist's school of thought is closely related to therapeutic effectiveness.

KEY: T F F F F T T F F T T F F T F

Chapter Fifteen Review

IDEAS: REVIEW OF LEARNING OBJECTIVES

When you have mastered the material in this chapter you should be able to do the following.

1.   Describe what encounter groups tend to be like.

2.   Summarize evidence on how participants are affected by encounter groups.

3.   Summarize evidence on factors which influence encounter group outcomes.

4.   Discuss why caution is advisable in seeking encounter group experiences.

5. Describe the nature and purpose of biofeedback systems.

6. Summarize evidence on biofeedback produced control of brain activity.

7. Briefly summarize the biofeedback work done on the control of cardiovascular activity, skin temperature, and muscle relaxation.

8. Describe hypnotic induction and discuss hypnotic susceptibility.

9. List 5 hypnotic phenomena mentioned in the text.

10. Explain the role-playing and altered consciousness theories of hypnosis.

11. Discuss practical applications of hypnosis.

12. Discuss precautions and limitations relative to the use of hypnosis.

13. Describe Transcendental Meditation and its alleged benefits.

14. Summarize research on TM.

15. Describe the Zen philosophy.

16. Summarize research on Zen.

17. Describe the practice of yoga.

18. Summarize research on yoga.

19. Describe <u>est</u>.

20. Describe Scientology.

21. Describe Silva Mind Control.

22. Summarize the text's critique of <u>est</u>, Scientology and Silva Mind Control.

23. List 5 guidelines recommended in pursuing self-improvement.

TERMS: REVIEW OF NEW VOCABULARY

Fill in the appropriate term for each definition.

Asanas   GSR device   Placebo effects
Biofeedback system   Hatha yoga   Pranayama
Charlatanism   Hypnosis   Satori
Electromyograph   Koan   Transcendental meditation
Encounter group   Mantra   Zen
Group therapy

_____   1. False claims to knowledge, skills and abilities.

_____   2. Group experience designed to promote personal
                            growth.

_____ 3. Physiological processes are monitored in order to aid a person in gaining control over them.

_____ 4. Device that measures muscle tension.

_____ 5. Technique which produces increased suggestibility and narrowed attention.

_____ 6. Westernized form of meditation.

_____ 7. Word used as focus of attention in TM.

_____ 8. Philosophy of life derived from Buddhism and Taoism.

_____ 9. In Zen, state of profound insight and awareness.

_____10. In Zen, paradoxical question.

_____11. Form of yoga that attempts to promote physical health.

_____12. Bodily postures used in yoga.

_____13. Breathing exercises used in yoga.

_____14. Device that measures galvanic skin response.

_____15. Change attributed to fake or ineffectual treatment.

PEOPLE: REVIEW OF MAJOR THEORISTS AND RESEARCHERS

Match the people with their contributions and/or ideas.

A. Werner Erhard

B. Ernest & Josephine Hilgard

C. Ron Hubbard

D. Lieberman, Yalom & Miles

E. Martin Orne

F. Jose Silva

G. Alan Watts

_____ 1. Research on encounter groups.

_____ 2. Research on hypnotic susceptibility.

_____ 3. Research on role-playing in hypnosis.

_____ 4. Promoted Zen philosophy in the West.

_____ 5. Creator of est.

_____ 6. Creator of Scientology.

_____ 7. Creator of Silva Mind Control.

SELF-TEST

Indicate whether the following statements are true or false and check your responses with the answer key below.

_____ 1. Encounter groups are used for the treatment of psychological disorders.

_____ 2. Encounter groups can be harmful to the participants.

_____ 3. Biofeedback can be used to train subjects to control their heart rate.

_____ 4.   People have been trained with biofeedback to control skin
            temperature in order to combat headaches.

_____ 5.   Not everyone can be hypnotized.

_____ 6.   Some hypnotic phenomena can be duplicated by non-hypnotized
            subjects.

_____ 7.   Evidence indicates that TM does not affect a person's
            physiological processes.

_____ 8.   Satori are breathing exercises used in yoga.

_____ 9.   Placebo effects may account for some of the success of
            systems such as est.

_____10.   In pursuing self-improvement, it is wise to jump in quickly
            or the opportunity may be missed forever.

KEY: F T T T T T F F T F

Part II
Introduction to the Personal Explorations Workbook

In your textbook, I repeatedly emphasize the great value of developing an accurate self-concept. Most theories of psychological health endorse the importance of forming a realistic picture of your personal qualities and capabilities. The *Personal Explorations Workbook* includes two kinds of exercises intended to help you in this endeavor. They are: (1) personal probes designed to make you analyze various aspects of your life, and (2) psychological tests or scales which you can take and score yourself.

PERSONAL PROBES

The personal probes consist of a set of questions intended to make you think about yourself. They involve systematic inquiries into: how you behave in certain situations, how your behavior has been shaped by past events, how you play certain roles, how you might improve yourself and so forth. The aspects of your life probed by these inquiries are, of course, tied to the content of the chapters in your text. You will probably derive the most benefit from them if you read the corresponding text chapter first.

PSYCHOLOGICAL SCALES

In addition to the Personal Probes, I have included eight psychological scales that are relevant to the topics covered in your text. Instructions are provided so that you can administer each scale to yourself, and then compute your score. After scoring the scale, you are given an explanation of what the scale measures. This is followed by a very brief review of research on the scale. These reviews concentrate primarily on reliability, validity, and how the scale attribute is related to other traits or behavioral tendencies. The final section for each test provides information to allow you to interpret the meaning of your score. Norms are supplied along with a description of what it means to obtain a high, intermediate or low score. Some of the explanatory material may be a bit too technical for some of you, but that should not prevent you from using the scales fruitfully. For example, I explain the norms for most of the scales in terms of standard deviations, a rather simple descriptive statistic. If you do not know what a standard deviation is,

you can glide right over this information. However, for those of you
who do know, I wanted to be quite explicit about the basis for the norms.
Many of you may have had courses in statistics and/or psychological
testing and may find this kind of information both necessary and
interesting. If it is too technical for you, you can ignore it without
having your use of the scales hampered in any way.

   It is hoped that you may gain some insight about yourself by responding
to these scales. However, you should be careful about attributing too
much significance to your scores. As I explain in the application
section of Chapter 2 in the text, caution is in order when interpreting
test results such as these. Most of the scales are self-report inventories. On such tests, your scores are only as accurate as the information that you provide in your responses. Thus it is important to:
(1) try to be candid, and (2) regard the results as interesting
"food for thought" rather than as a definitive statement about your
personality or abilities. To make appropriate use of this feature in
your workbook, you should definitely read the application section for
Chapter 2 in your text even if it is not assigned by your instructor.

   Although the various scales can stand on their own, they will be most
valuable if they are used in conjunction with the chapters specified.
For each scale I indicate which chapters in your book are related to
the trait or attribute being measured. You will find your test results
more interesting if you have read the relevant chapters.

   Finally, I must emphasize again that these exercises will only be as
valuable as you make them, by trying very hard to respond honestly.
Usually, respondents do not know what a scale measures when they are
taking it. The conventional approach is to put some "bogus" title at
the top of the scale, such as "Biographical Inventory." I have not
bothered doing this since you could easily find out what any scale
measures simply by turning a page or two. Thus, you will be taking
each scale with some idea (based on the title) of what the scale
measures. The thing to remember is that these scales are included for
your personal edification. They are intended to satisfy your
curiosity. There is no reason to try to impress or mislead anyone
(including yourself). Your results will be accurate and meaningful only
if you try very, very hard to respond in a candid manner.

Why Did I Take This Course?

1. What led you to enroll in this particular course?

2. Have you taken other psychology courses? If yes, which courses,
    and did you enjoy them?

3. What do you expect to get out of this course? What are your
    goals?

4.   Have you read any "self-help" books? If yes, list some.

5.   Do you think that you gained anything from reading any of these "self-help" books?

6.   How do you feel about school (bored, threatened, excited and so forth)?

Name _____

Who Am I?

1. Below you will find 75 personality-trait words taken from the list
   assembled by Anderson (1968). Try to select the 20 traits (20 only!)
   that describe you best. Check them.

sincere	pessimistic	open-minded
suspicious	patient	tense
cooperative	neat	logical
vain	sociable	scornful
cheerful	honest	reasonable
forgetful	crafty	methodical
sly	headstrong	naive
sloppy	grouchy	ethical
persuasive	nervous	clumsy
rebellious	studious	understanding
truthful	mature	skeptical
efficient	resourceful	perceptive
punctual	prejudiced	friendly
gracious	shy	short-tempered
compulsive	sarcastic	respectful
imaginative	impolite	diligent
prideful	optimistic	considerate
courteous	candid	idealistic
warm	versatile	courageous
tactful	loyal	reliable
outgoing	dependable	persistent
orderly	energetic	modest
smart	kind	good-humored
unselfish	cordial	wholesome
generous	boastful	daring

2. Review the 20 traits that you chose. Overall, is it a favorable
   or unfavorable picture that you have sketched?

3. Considering Carl Rogers' point, that we often distort reality and
    construct an overly favorable self-concept, do you feel that you
    were objective?

4. What characteristics make you unique?

5. What are your greatest strengths?

6. What are your greatest weaknesses?

Name _____

Where's the Stress in My Life?

1. As you learned in Chapter 3, it's a good idea to be aware of the stress in your life. For this exercise you should keep a stress awareness record for one week. Take this sheet with you and about twice a day, fill in the information on any stressful events that have occurred. Under "types of stress" indicate whether the event involves frustration, conflict, pressure, change or some combination.

Day	Time	Stressful Event	Type of Stress	Your Reaction

At the end of the week, answer the following questions.

2. Is there a particular type of stress that is most frequent in your life?

3. Is there a particular locale or set of responsibilities that produces a great deal of stress for you?

4. Are there certain reactions to stressful events that you display consistently?

5. Is there anything reasonable that you could do to reduce the amount of stress in your life?

Name _____

Can I Learn to Detect Irrational Thinking?

You should begin this exercise by reviewing the theories of Albert Ellis covered in Chapter 4 of your text. To briefly recapitulate, Ellis believes that unpleasant emotional reactions are caused not by events themselves, but by irrational interpretations of events derived from irrational assumptions. It is therefore important to detect and dispute these irrational modes of thinking. Over a period of a week or so, see if you can spot three examples of irrational thinking on your part. Describe these examples as requested below.

Example No. 1

Activating event:

Irrational self-talk:

Consequent emotional reaction:

Irrational assumption producing irrational thought:

More rational, alternative view:

Example No. 2

Activating event:

Irrational self-talk:

Consequent emotional reaction:

Irrational assumption producing irrational thought:

More rational, alternative view:

Example No. 3

Activating event:

Irrational self-talk:

Consequent emotional reaction:

Irrational assumption producing irrational thought:

More rational, alternative view:

How Can I Use Self-Modification to Change My Behavior?

After reading Chapter 5, you should understand that self-modification procedures can be very valuable in improving self-control. This exercise is intended to see if you can skillfully apply the principles of self-modification discussed in your text. Your task is to design and execute a self-modification program that will alter some aspect of your behavior.

Step One: Specifying the target behavior. List below the target behavior or behaviors that you would like to modify. Indicate whether you will increase or decrease their frequency.

Step Two: Gathering baseline data. Summarize below the kinds of data that you will need to collect during your baseline period. What will be the length of your baseline period? List any consistent antecedents or consequences of your target response(s) that you discovered in collecting your baseline data.

Step Three: Designing the program. Summarize below your intervention strategies.

Reinforcers to be used.

Reinforcement contingencies.

Antecedents to be controlled.

Other procedures used.

Step Four: Executing and evaluating your program. After executing your program for at least 3 weeks, describe how well it worked. Mention any problems that surfaced or any adjustments that had to be made. You may want to attach charts which graph your progress in altering your behavior.

Step Five: Ending your program. Summarize how (or whether) you plan to phase out your program.

Name _____

How Does My Self-Concept Compare to My Self/Ideal?

Below you will find a list of 15 personal attributes, each portrayed on a 9-point continuum. Mark with an X where you think you fall on each attribute. Try to be candid and accurate; these marks will collectively describe a portion of your self-concept. When you are finished with the above task, go back and circle where you wish you could be on each dimension. These marks describe your self-ideal. Finally, in the spaces on the right, indicate the size of the discrepancy (between self-concept and self-ideal) for each attribute.

1. Decisive   Indecisive
    9   8   7   6   5   4   3   2   1   _____

2. Anxious   Relaxed
    9   8   7   6   5   4   3   2   1   _____

3. Easily influenced   Independent thinker
    9   8   7   6   5   4   3   2   1   _____

4. Very intelligent   Less intelligent
    9   8   7   6   5   4   3   2   1   _____

5. In good physical shape   In poor physical shape
    9   8   7   6   5   4   3   2   1   _____

6. Undependable   Dependable
    9   8   7   6   5   4   3   2   1   _____

7. Deceitful   Honest
    9   8   7   6   5   4   3   2   1   _____

8. A leader   A follower
    9   8   7   6   5   4   3   2   1   _____

9. Unambitious   Ambitious
    9   8   7   6   5   4   3   2   1   _____

10. Self-confident   Insecure
    9   8   7   6   5   4   3   2   1   _____

11. Conservative   Adventurous
    9   8   7   6   5   4   3   2   1   _____

12. Extroverted   Introverted
    9   8   7   6   5   4   3   2   1   _____

13. Physically attractive   Physically unattractive
    9   8   7   6   5   4   3   2   1   _____

14. Lazy   Hardworking
    9   8   7   6   5   4   3   2   1   _____

15. Funny   Little sense of humor
    9   8   7   6   5   4   3   2   1   _____

1. Overall, how would you describe the discrepancy between your self-concept and your self-ideal (large, moderate, small, large on a few dimensions and so forth)?

2. How do sizable gaps in any of your attributes affect your self-esteem?

3. Do you feel that any of the gaps exist because you have had others' ideals imposed on you or because you have thoughtlessly accepted other's ideals?

4. Identify several attributes that you realistically feel can be changed to narrow the gap between your self-concept and your self-ideal.

How Do I Feel about Self-Disclosure?

You should be aware of the importance of self-disclosure in communication after reading Chapter 7. This exercise is intended to make you think about your self-disclosure behavior. Begin by finishing the incomplete sentences below (adapted from Egan, 1977). Go through the sentences fairly quickly; do not ponder your responses too long. There are no right or wrong answers.

1. I dislike people who. . .

2. Those who really know me. . .

3. When I let someone know something I don't like about myself. . .

4. When I'm in a group of strangers. . .

5. I envy. . .

6. I get hurt when. . .

7. I daydream about. . .

8. Few people know that I. . .

9. One thing I really dislike about myself is. . .

10. When I share my values with someone. . .

1. Based on your responses to the incomplete sentences, do you feel you engage in the right amount of self-disclosure? Too little? Too much?

2. In general, what prevents you from engaging in self-disclosure?

3. Are there particular topics on which you find it difficult to be self-disclosing?

4. Are you the recipient of much self-disclosure from others, or do people have difficulty opening up to you?

What Are My Attitudes on Sex-Roles?

1. Considering the stereotypes outlined in Table 8.1 in your text, would you characterize yourself as feminine, masculine or andro-gynous?

2. Did your parents model traditional sex-roles or did they deviate some from the norm?

3. Can you recall any experiences that were particularly influential in shaping your sex-role attitudes? If yes, give a couple of examples.

4. Were you ever encouraged to engage in cross sex-typed behavior?
    Can you think of a couple of examples?

5. Do you ever feel restricted by sex-roles?

6. Have you ever been a victim of sex discrimination (sexism)?

7. How do you think the transition in sex-roles has affected you
    personally?

How Do I Relate to Friends?

The following questions (adapted from Egan, 1979) are designed to make
you think about how you deal with friendships.

1. Do I have many friends or very few?

2. Whether many or few, do I usually spend a lot of time with my
    friends?

3. What do I like in other people - that is, what makes me choose them
    as friends?

4. Are the people I go around with like me or different from me?
    Or are they in some ways like me and in other ways different?
    How?

5. Do I play games with others, or do I prefer to be straightforward and direct with them? Do people play games with me?

6. Do I like to control others, to get them to do things my way? Do I let others control me? Do I give in to others much of the time?

7. Are there ways in which my friendships are one-sided?

8. Am I willing to allow others to be themselves?

How Do I Behave in Intimate Relationships?

The following questions (adapted from Corey, 1978) are intended to make you think about how you act in intimate relationships. They are designed for people in "couple-type" relationships, but if you are not currently involved in one, you can apply them to whatever relationship is most significant in your life presently (for instance, with your parents, children or best friend).

1. What are some sources of conflict in your relationship? Check any of the following items that apply to you, and list any other areas of conflict in the space provided.

    _____ spending money

    _____ use of free time

    _____ what to do about boredom

    _____ investment of energy in work

    _____ interest in others of the opposite sex

    _____ outside friendships

    _____ wanting children

    _____ how to deal with children

    _____ differences in basic values

    _____ in-laws

    _____ sexual needs and satisfaction

    _____ expression of caring and loving

    _____ power struggles

    _____ role conflicts

    _____ others (list below)

2. How do you generally cope with these conflicts in your relationship?
    Check the items that most apply to you.

    _____ by open dialogue
    _____ by avoidance
    _____ by fighting and arguing
    _____ by compromising
    _____ by getting involved with other people or in projects

    List other ways in which you deal with conflicts in your relationship:

3. Mention one conflict that you would like to resolve, and write down
    what you'd be willing to do in order to help resolve it.

    The conflict is:

    To attempt a resolution, I'm willing to:

4. List some ways in which you've changed during the period of your
    relationship. How have your changes affected the relationship?

5. How much do you need (and depend upon) the other person? Imagine
    that he or she is no longer in your life, and write down how your
    life might be different.

How Did I Acquire My Attitudes on Sex?

1. Who do your feel was most important in shaping your attitudes regarding sexual behavior (parents, teachers, peers, early girl-friend or boyfriend, and so forth)?

2. What was the nature of their influence?

3. If the answer to the first question was not your parents, what kind of information did you get at home? Were your parents comfortable talking about sex?

4. In childhood, were you ever made to feel shameful, guilty or fearful about sex? How?

5. Were you ever punished for being caught in some kind of sex play when you were young?

6. Were your parents open or secretive about their own sex lives?

7. Do you feel comfortable with your sexuality today?

What Do I Know about the Career/Vocation That Interests Me?

Important vocational decisions require <u>information</u>. Your assignment in this exercise is to pick a vocation and research it. You should begin by reading some occupational literature (consult your text for some suggestions). Then you should interview someone in the field. Use the outline below to summarize your findings.

1. <u>The nature of the work.</u> What are your duties and responsibilities on a day-to-day basis?

2. <u>Working conditions.</u> Is the working environment pleasant or unpleasant, low-key or high-pressure?

3. <u>Job entry requirements.</u> What kind of education and training are required to break into this occupational area?

4. Potential earnings. What are entry-level salaries and how much can you hope to earn if you're exceptionally successful? What does the average person earn? What are the fringe benefits?

5. Potential status. What is the social status associated with this occupation? Is it personally satisfactory for you?

6. Opportunities for advancement. How do you "move up" in this field? Are there adequate opportunities for promotion and advancement?

7. Intrinsic job satisfactions. Outside of money and formal fringe benefits, what can you derive in the way of personal satisfaction from this job? Will it allow you to have fun, help people, be creative, or shoulder responsibility?

8. Future outlook. How is supply and demand projected to shape up in the future for this occupational area?

Name _____

What Are My Attitudes toward People with Psychological Disorders?

1. List 7 adjectives that you associate with people who are diagnosed as mentally ill.

2. When you meet people that you know were once diagnosed as mentally ill, what are your immediate reactions?

3. List some comments about people with psychological disorders that you heard when you were a child.

4. Have you had any actual interactions with "mentally ill people" that have supported or contradicted your expectations?

5. Do you agree with the idea that psychological disorders should be viewed as an illness or disease? Defend your position.

What Are My Feelings about Professional Psychotherapy?

The following questions (adapted from Corey, 1978) are intended to make you examine your attitudes regarding professional psychotherapy.

1. If you have had any experience with mental health professionals, describe what it was like.

2. Based on your experience, would you recommend professional counseling to a friend?

3. List any considerations that might prevent you from seeking some form of therapy even if you felt a need or desire to do so.

4. If you were looking for a therapist, what criteria would you employ in making your choice?

5. Briefly describe what you would expect to get out of professional therapy or counseling.

What New Approach to Personal Growth Would I Like to Explore?

Throughout your text you have been exposed to a great variety of approaches to personal growth and self-improvement. In particular, in Chapter 15 we introduced many esoteric or "off-beat" approaches. Your assignment in this last exercise is to select some growth system that you are not already familiar with, and go to an introductory lecture or session. Many of these growth systems offer introductions for free or for a nominal fee. Some suggestions are mentioned below, but don't limit yourself to this list.

Yoga	Meditation training
Assertiveness training	Zen training
Peer self-help group	Hypnosis
Women's consciousness raising group	Est
Encounter group	Scientology
Relaxation training	Silva mind control
Coping skills training	Time management workshop
Sensitivity training	Biofeedback

After visiting an introductory session, answer the following questions.

1. Describe the personal growth/self-improvement system that you learned about in your introductory session.

2. What is the cost for getting the full training course or instruction?

3. What are the benefits of this personal growth/self-improvement system?

4. Did you ever feel in your introductory session that the possible benefits were being exaggerated?

5. Were the trainers/leaders realistic and candid about how much effort and work would be required to gain the possible benefits of this approach to growth?

6. Were the trainers/leaders professional or were there some overtones of charlatanism?

7. Are you interested in pursuing this approach to personal growth further? Why?

Sensation-Seeking Scale

For use with Chapters 2, 3 or 5.

INSTRUCTIONS

Each of the items below contains two choices, A and B. Please indicate in the spaces provided on the left which of the choices most describes your likes or the way you feel. In some cases you may find items in which both choices describe your likes or the way you feel. Please choose the one which better describes your likes or feelings. In some cases you may find items in which you do not like either choice. In these cases mark the choice you dislike least. It is important you respond to all items with only one choice, A or B. We are interested only in your likes or feelings, not in how others feel about these things or how one is supposed to feel. There are no right or wrong answers as in other kinds of tests. Be frank and give your honest appraisal of yourself.

THE SCALE

_____ 1. A. I would like a job which would require a lot of traveling.
       B. I would prefer a job in one location.

_____ 2. A. I am invigorated by a brisk, cold day.
       B. I can't wait to get into the indoors on a cold day.

_____ 3. A. I find a certain pleasure in routine kinds of work.
       B. Although it is sometimes necessary I usually dislike routine kinds of work.

_____ 4. A. I often wish I could be a mountain climber.
       B. I can't understand people who risk their necks climbing mountains.

_____ 5. A. I dislike all body odors.
       B. I like some of the earthy body smells.

_____ 6. A. I get bored seeing the same old faces.
       B. I like the comfortable familiarity of everyday friends.

_____ 7.   A.   I like to explore a strange city or section of town by myself, even if it means getting lost.
       B.   I prefer a guide when I am in a place I don't know well.

_____ 8.   A.   I find the quickest and easiest route to a place and stick to it.
       B.   I sometimes take different routes to a place I often go, just for variety's sake.

_____ 9.   A.   I would not like to try any drug which might produce strange and dangerous effects on me.
       B.   I would like to try some of the new drugs that produce hallucinations.

_____ 10. A.   I would prefer living in an ideal society where everyone is safe, secure, and happy.
       B.   I would have preferred living in the unsettled days of our history.

_____ 11. A.   I sometimes like to do things that are a little frightening.
       B.   A sensible person avoids activities that are dangerous.

_____ 12. A.   I order the dishes with which I am familiar, so as to avoid disappointment and unpleasantness.
       B.   I like to try new foods that I have never tasted before.

_____ 13. A.   I can't stand riding with a person who likes to speed.
       B.   I sometimes like to drive very fast because I find it exciting.

_____ 14. A.   If I were a salesman I would prefer a straight salary, rather than the risk of making little or nothing on a commission basis.
       B.   If I were a salesman I would prefer working on a commission if I had a chance to make more money than I could on a salary.

_____ 15. A.   I would like to take up the sport of water skiing.
       B.   I would not like to take up the sport of water skiing.

_____ 16. A.   I don't like to argue with people whose beliefs are sharply divergent from mine, since such arguments are never resolved.
       B.   I find people that disagree with my beliefs more stimulating than people who agree with me.

_____ 17. A.   When I go on a trip I like to plan my route and timetable fairly carefully.
       B.   I would like to take off on a trip with no preplanned or definite routes, or timetables.

_____ 18. A.   I enjoy the thrills of watching car races.
       B.   I find car races unpleasant.

_____ 19. A.   Most people spend entirely too much money on life insurance.
       B.   Life insurance is something that no man can afford to be without.

_____ 20. A. I would like to learn to fly an airplane.
       B. I would not like to learn to fly an airplane.

_____ 21. A. I would not like to be hypnotized.
       B. I would like to have the experience of being hypnotized.

_____ 22. A. The most important goal of life is to live it to the fullest
          and experience as much of it as you can.
       B. The most important goal of life is to find peace and
          happiness.

_____ 23. A. I would like to try parachute jumping.
       B. I would never want to try jumping out of a plane, with or
          without a parachute.

_____ 24. A. I enter cold water gradually giving myself time to get
          used to it.
       B. I like to dive or jump right into the ocean or a cold pool.

_____ 25. A. I do not like the irregularity and discord of most modern
          music.
       B. I like to listen to new and unusual kinds of music.

_____ 26. A. I prefer friends who are excitingly unpredictable.
       B. I prefer friends who are reliable and predictable.

_____ 27. A. When I go on a vacation I prefer the comfort of a good room
          and bed.
       B. When I go on a vacation I would prefer the change of camp-
          ing out.

_____ 28. A. The essence of good art is in its clarity, symmetry of
          form, and harmony of colors.
       B. I often find beauty in the "clashing" colors and irregular
          forms of modern paintings.

_____ 29. A. The worst social sin is to be rude.
       B. The worst social sin is to be a bore.

_____ 30. A. I look forward to a good night of rest after a long day.
       B. I wish I didn't have to waste so much of a day sleeping.

_____ 31. A. I prefer people who are emotionally expressive even if
          they are a bit unstable.
       B. I prefer people who are calm and even tempered.

_____ 32. A. A good painting should shock or jolt the senses.
       B. A good painting should give one a feeling of peace and
          security.

_____ 33. A. When I feel discouraged I recover by relaxing and having
          some soothing diversion.
       B. When I feel discouraged I recover by going out and doing
          something new and exciting.

_____ 34. A. People who ride motorcycles must have some kind of an
          unconscious need to hurt themselves.
       B. I would like to drive or ride on a motorcycle.

SCORING THE SCALE

The scoring key is reproduced below. You should circle your response of A or B each time it corresponds to the keyed response below. Add up the number of responses you circle, and this total is your score on the Sensation-Seeking Scale. Record your score below.

1.	A	8.	B	15.	A	22.	A	29.	B
2.	A	9.	B	16.	B	23.	A	30.	B
3.	B	10.	B	17.	B	24.	B	31.	A
4.	A	11.	A	18.	A	25.	B	32.	A
5.	B	12.	B	19.	A	26.	A	33.	B
6.	A	13.	B	20.	A	27.	B	34.	B
7.	A	14.	B	21.	B	28.	B		

MY SCORE _____

WHAT THE SCALE MEASURES

As its name implies, the Sensation-Seeking Scale (SSS) measures one's need for a high level of stimulation. As discussed in your text (see Box 3.6), sensation-seeking involves the active pursuit of experiences which many people would find very stressful. Marvin Zuckerman (1979) believes that this thirst for sensation is a general personality trait that leads people to seek thrills, adventures and new experiences.

RESEARCH ON THE SCALE

The scale which you just responded to is the second version of the SSS. Test-retest reliabilities are quite respectable and there is minimal contamination by social desirability bias. There is ample evidence to support the scale's validity. For example, studies show that high sensation-seekers appraise hypothetical situations as less risky than low sensation-seekers and are more willing to volunteer for an experiment in which they will be hypnotized. The scale also shows robust positive correlations with measures of change-seeking, novelty seeking, extraversion and impulsiveness. Interestingly, SSS scores tend to decline with increasing age.

INTERPRETING YOUR SCORE

Our norms are based on percentiles reported by Zuckerman and colleagues for a sample of 62 undergraduates. Although males generally tend to score a bit higher than females on the SSS, the differences are small enough to report one set of (averaged) norms. Remember, sensation-seeking scores tend to decline with age. So, if you're not in the modal college student age range (17-23) these norms may be a bit high.

Norms

High Score:	20-34	(roughly more than 1 standard deviation above the mean)
Intermediate Score:	11-20	(within 1 standard deviation of the mean either way)
Low Score:	0-10	(roughly more than 1 standard deviation below the mean)

High Scorers: You thrive on sensation. You probably are easily bored and need to be challenged. People such as yourself satisfy their need for stimulation by seeking adventures, taking risks, pursuing unusual experiences (such as hypnosis or meditation), partying, gambling, traveling frequently, experimenting with drugs and so forth. While you may not be drawn to all of the above activities, you nonetheless are quite likely to be bored by routine; you have a thirst for new and different activities, whatever they may be.

Intermediate Scorers: A score in this range suggests that you are roughly average in sensation-seeking. Although you probably do not go out of your way to avoid high stimulation, you probably don't pursue it obsessively either.

Low Scorers: A low score means that you generally find high levels of stimulation to be aversive. The experiences that high sensation-seekers crave do not appeal to you. In fact, you may find them threatening and you may be mystified by others' flirtation with danger. You probably feel comfortable with routine and value security highly. Thrill seeking just isn't your cup of tea.

Locus of Control Scale

For use with Chapters 2, 3 or 6.

INSTRUCTIONS

   Answer the following questions the way you feel. There are no right
or wrong answers. Don't take too much time answering any one question,
but do try to answer them all. One of your concerns during the test
may be, "What should I do if I can answer both yes and no to a
question?" It's not unusual for that to happen. If it does, think
about whether your answer is just a little more one way than the other.
For example, if you'd assign a weighting of 51 percent to "yes" and
assign 49 percent to "no," mark the answer "yes." Try to pick one or
the other response for all questions and not leave any blank. Mark your
response to the question in the space provided on the left.

THE SCALE

_____ 1. Do you believe that most problems will solve themselves if you
          just don't fool with them?

_____ 2. Do you believe that you can stop yourself from catching a cold?

_____ 3. Are some people just born lucky?

_____ 4. Most of the time do you feel that getting good grades meant a
          great deal to you?

_____ 5. Are you often blamed for things that just aren't your fault?

_____ 6. Do you believe that if somebody studies hard enough he or she
          can pass any subject?

_____ 7. Do you feel that most of the time it doesn't pay to try hard
          because things never turn out right anyway?

_____ 8. Do you feel that if things start out well in the morning that
          it's going to be a good day no matter what you do?

_____ 9. Do you feel that most of the time parents listen to what their
          children have to say?

_____ 10. Do you believe that wishing can make good things happen?

_____ 11. When you get punished does it usually seem it's for no good
          reason at all?

_____12.   Most of the time do you find it hard to change a friend's (mind) opinion?

_____13.   Do you think that cheering more than luck helps a team to win?

_____14.   Did you feel that it was nearly impossible to change your parent's mind about anything?

_____15.   Do you believe that parents should allow children to make most of their own decisions?

_____16.   Do you feel that when you do something wrong there's very little you can do to make it right?

_____17.   Do you believe that most people are just born good at sports?

_____18.   Are most of the other people your age stronger than you are?

_____19.   Do you feel that one of the best ways to handle most problems is just not to think about them?

_____20.   Do you feel that you have a lot of choice in deciding whom your friends are?

_____21.   If you find a four leaf clover, do you believe that it might bring you good luck?

_____22.   Did you often feel that whether or not you did your homework had much to do with what kind of grades you got?

_____23.   Do you feel that when a person your age is angry at you, there's little you can do to stop him or her?

_____24.   Have you ever had a good luck charm?

_____25.   Do you believe that whether or not people like you depends on how you act?

_____26.   Did your parents usually help you if you asked them to?

_____27.   Have you felt that when people were angry with you it was usually for no reason at all?

_____28.   Most of the time, do you feel that you can change what might happen tomorrow by what you do today?

_____29.   Do you believe that when bad things are going to happen they just are going to happen no matter what you try to do to stop them?

_____30.   Do you think that people can get their own way if they just keep trying?

_____31.   Most of the time do you find it useless to try to get your own way at home?

_____32.   Do you feel that when good things happen they happen because of hard work?

_____33.   Do you feel that when somebody your age wants to be your enemy there's little you can do to change matters?

_____34.   Do you feel that it's easy to get friends to do what you want them to do?

_____35. Do you usually feel that you have little to say about what you get to eat at home?

_____36. Do you feel that when someone doesn't like you there's little you can do about it?

_____37. Did you usually feel that it was almost useless to try in school because most other children were just plain smarter than you were?

_____38. Are you the kind of person who believes that planning ahead makes things turn out better?

_____39. Most of the time do you feel that you have little to say about what your family decides to do?

_____40. Do you think it's better to be smart than to be lucky?

SCORING THE SCALE

The scoring key is reproduced below. You should circle your yes or no response each time it corresponds to the keyed response below. Add up the number of responses you circle, and this total is your score on the Locus of Control Scale. Record your score below.

1.	Yes	9.	No	17.	Yes	25.	No	33.	Yes
2.	No	10.	Yes	18.	Yes	26.	No	34.	No
3.	Yes	11.	Yes	19.	Yes	27.	Yes	35.	Yes
4.	No	12.	Yes	20.	No	28.	No	36.	Yes
5.	Yes	13.	No	21.	Yes	29.	Yes	37.	Yes
6.	No	14.	Yes	22.	No	30.	No	38.	No
7.	Yes	15.	No	23.	Yes	31.	Yes	39.	Yes
8.	Yes	16.	Yes	24.	Yes	32.	No	40.	No

MY SCORE _____

WHAT THE SCALE MEASURES

Locus of control is a personality dimension originally described by Julian Rotter (1966). According to Rotter, people vary in regard to how responsible they feel for their own fate. Individuals with an internal locus of control tend to believe that people are responsible for their successes and failures. Conversely, people with a relatively external locus of control tend to attribute successes and failures to luck, chance or fate. The scale you just responded to was developed by Stephen Nowicki and Marshall Duke (1974) in order to remedy some technical problems that were characteristic of the original Rotter (1966) scale. Like the original, it measures one's belief about whether events are controlled internally or externally.

RESEARCH ON THE SCALE

Reports on test-retest reliability (Chandler, 1976; Nowicki & Duke, 1974) have yielded very respectable figures (such as .83 over a six-week period). While the original Rotter (1966) scale was plagued by a tendency for subjects to give socially desirable responses, the Nowicki and Duke version seems to have minimized this problem. The validity of the scale has been supported by evidence that it correlates well with the original Rotter scale, and that it is related to other variables in the same way that the original scale was.

Locus of control has been related to a wide range of variables. One of the more interesting is race. Generally, Blacks score more toward the external end than do Whites (Duke & Nowicki, 1972). Presumably, this is because Blacks are more likely to be victims of discrimination wherein they do not get rewards that they feel that they have earned. There is also evidence that external locus of control is related weakly to neuroticism and anxiety. Internal locus of control has been shown to be associated with greater academic achievement.

INTERPRETING YOUR SCORE

Our norms are based on data collected by Nowicki and Duke (1974) for 154 Caucasian college students. Additional studies suggest that Blacks and other ethnic minorities should probably shift the score cutoffs upward by about five points.

Norms

External Score:	16-40	(more than 1.50 standard deviations above the mean)
Intermediate Score:	7-15	(from 0.75 standard deviations below the mean up to 1.50 standard deviations above the mean)
Internal Score:	0-6	(more than 0.75 standard deviations below the mean)

External Scorers: A score above 15 suggests that you have a fairly strong belief that events are beyond your control. In other words, you do not feel that there is much of a connection between your behavior and your outcomes. As discussed in Chapter 6 of your text, this means that you are relatively less likely than others to take credit for your successes or to take the blame for your failures. Instead, you tend to believe that success and failure are primarily a matter of luck and chance breaks.

Intermediate Scorers: A score in this range means that you have inconsistent views about the degree to which you control your own fate. You probably believe that you do control your own fate in some areas of your life, while believing that you have little control in other areas.

Internal Scorers: A score below 7 indicates that you have a firm belief in your ability to influence your outcomes. Your relatively internal score means that you generally do not attribute your successes and failures to good and bad luck or chance factors. Instead, you feel that you can influence the course of what happens to you. As mentioned in Chapter 3 of your text, an internal locus of control is associated with relatively great stress tolerance.

Name _____

Self-Control Schedule

For use with Chapters 4 or 5.

INSTRUCTIONS

Indicate how characteristic or descriptive each of the following statements is of you by using the code given below.

+3 very characteristic of me, extremely descriptive
+2 rather characteristic of me, quite descriptive
+1 somewhat characteristic of me, slightly descriptive
-1 somewhat uncharacteristic of me, slightly undescriptive
-2 rather uncharacteristic of me, quite undescriptive
-3 very uncharacteristic of me, extremely nondescriptive

Record your responses in the spaces provided on the left.

THE SCALE

_____ 1. When I do a boring job, I think about the less boring parts of the job and the reward that I will receive once I am finished.

_____ 2. When I have to do something that is anxiety arousing for me, I try to visualize how I will overcome my anxieties while doing it.

_____ 3. Often by changing my way of thinking I am able to change my feelings about almost everything.

_____ 4. I often find it difficult to overcome my feelings of nervousness and tension without any outside help.

_____ 5. When I am feeling depressed I try to think about pleasant events.

_____ 6. I cannot avoid thinking about mistakes I have made in the past.

_____ 7. When I am faced with a difficult problem, I try to approach its solution in a systematic way.

_____ 8. I usually do my duties quicker when somebody is pressuring me.

_____ 9. When I am faced with a difficult decision, I prefer to postpone making a decision even if all the facts are at my disposal.

_____ 10. When I find that I have difficulties in concentrating on my reading, I look for ways to increase my concentration.

_____ 11. After I plan to work, I remove all the things that are not relevant to my work.

_____ 12. When I try to get rid of a bad habit, I first try to find out all the factors that maintain this habit.

_____ 13. When an unpleasant thought is bothering me, I try to think about something pleasant.

_____ 14. If I would smoke two packages of cigarettes a day, I probably would need outside help to stop smoking.

_____ 15. When I am in a low mood, I try to act cheerful so my mood will change.

_____ 16. If I had the pills with me, I would take a tranquilizer whenever I felt tense and nervous.

_____ 17. When I am depressed, I try to keep myself busy with things that I like.

_____ 18. I tend to postpone unpleasant duties even if I could perform them immediately.

_____ 19. I need outside help to get rid of some of my bad habits.

_____ 20. When I find it difficult to settle down and do a certain job, I look for ways to help me settle down.

_____ 21. Although it makes me feel bad, I cannot avoid thinking about all kinds of possible catastrophes in the future.

_____ 22. First of all I prefer to finish a job that I have to do and then start doing the things I really like.

_____ 23. When I feel pain in a certain part of my body, I try not to think about it.

_____ 24. My self-esteem increases once I am able to overcome a bad habit.

_____ 25. In order to overcome bad feelings that accompany failure, I often tell myself that it is not so catastrophic, and that I can do something about it.

_____ 26. When I feel that I am too impulsive, I tell myself "stop and think before you do anything."

_____ 27. Even when I am terribly angry at somebody, I consider my actions very carefully.

_____ 28. Facing the need to make a decision, I usually find out all the possible alternatives instead of deciding quickly and spontaneously.

_____ 29. Usually, I do first the things I really like to do even if there are more urgent things to do.

_____ 30. When I realize that I cannot help but be late for an important meeting, I tell myself to keep calm.

_____ 31. When I feel pain in my body, I try to divert my thoughts from it.

_____ 32. I usually plan my work when faced with a number of things to do.

_____ 33. When I am short of money, I decide to record all my expenses in order to plan carefully for the future.

_____ 34. If I find it difficult to concentrate on a certain job, I divide the job into smaller segments.

_____ 35. Quite often I cannot overcome unpleasant thoughts that bother me.

_____ 36. Once I am hungry and unable to eat, I try to divert my thoughts away from my stomach or try to imagine that I am satisfied.

SCORING THE SCALE

The items listed below are reverse-scored items. Thus, for each of them you should go back and simply change the + or - sign in front of the number you recorded.

4	9	18	29
6	14	19	35
8	16	21	

After making your reversals, all you need to do is add up the numbers you recorded for each of the 36 items. Of course, it is important to pay close attention to the algebraic sign in front of each number. The total you arrive at is your score on the Self-Control Schedule (SCS). Record your score below.

MY SCORE _____

WHAT THE SCALE MEASURES

Developed by Michael Rosenbaum (1980), the Self-Control Schedule assesses your ability to employ self-management methods to solve common behavioral problems. Specifically, it measures your tendency to: (1) use rational self-talk to modify emotional responses, (2) use systematic problem-solving strategies, and (3) delay immediate gratification when necessary. It also measures your perceptions regarding your self-control skills.

RESEARCH ON THE SCALE

Rosenbaum (1980) administered the SCS to a diversified batch of six samples including both student and non-student populations, many of them from Israel (Rosenbaum is affiliated with the University of Haifa). Test-retest reliability (.86 for four weeks) and internal reliability were found to be satisfactory. Support for the validity of the scale was derived from evidence that it correlates negatively with established measures of irrational thinking and external locus of control. Additional supportive evidence was garnered in an experimental study wherein high scorers on the SCS showed better self-control on a laboratory task than did low scorers.

INTERPRETING YOUR SCORE

Our norms are based on an American sample of 111 undergraduate students studied by Rosenbaum (1980). Although females tend to score a little higher on the scale than do males, the difference is not large enough to merit separate norms (so their means have been averaged).

Norms

High score:	Above 48	(more than 1 standard deviation above the mean)
Intermediate score:	6-47	(within 1 standard deviation of the mean either way)
Low score:	below 6	(more than 1 standard deviation below the mean, including negative scores)

High scorers: A high score suggests that you make extensive use of self-control strategies. A score in this category means that you already use the advice of Albert Ellis (see Chapter 4 in your text) about thinking rationally to shortcircuit potentially harmful emotional reactions. It also means that you have what Freud would have called ego strength - the ability to inhibit the temptation to always go for immediate gratification. Furthermore, you use systematic problem-solving strategies (see Chapter 4 again) and you have confidence in your self-control.

Intermediate scorers: A score in this bracket suggests that you are roughly average in the ability to maintain self-control. Since the SCS assesses four related but separate aspects of behavior, you may be strong in some areas and weak in others. You might want to review the four aspects of behavior assessed by the scale (described under "What the Scale Measures") and try to figure out which areas you are weak in.

Low scorers: A low score suggests that your self-control is minimal. This is unfortunate in that self-control is a key element in constructive coping. You can probably profit from the advice in your text on emotional self-control (Chapter 4), systematic problem solving (Chapter 4) and self-modification (Chapter 5).

Name _____

Self-Monitoring Scale

For use with Chapters 6 and 7

INSTRUCTIONS

The statements below concern your personal reactions to a number of different situations. No two statements are exactly alike so consider each statement carefully before answering. If a statement is true or mostly true as applied to you mark true as your answer. If a statement is false or not usually true as applied to you mark false as your answer. It is important that you answer as frankly and as honestly as you can. Record your responses in the spaces provided on the left.

THE SCALE

_____ 1. I find it hard to imitate the behavior of other people.

_____ 2. My behavior is usually an expression of my true inner feelings, attitudes and beliefs.

_____ 3. At parties and social gatherings, I do not attempt to do or say things that others will like.

_____ 4. I can only argue for ideas which I already believe.

_____ 5. I can make impromptu speeches even on topics about which I have almost no information.

_____ 6. I guess I put on a show to impress or entertain people.

_____ 7. When I am uncertain how to act in a social situation, I look to the behavior of others for cues.

_____ 8. I would probably make a good actor.

_____ 9. I rarely need the advice of my friends to choose movies, books or music.

_____10. I sometimes appear to others to be experiencing deeper emotions than I actually am.

_____11. I laugh more when I watch a comedy with others than when alone.

_____12. In a group of people I am rarely the center of attention.

_____13. In different situations and with different people, I often act like very different persons.

_____14. I am not particularly good at making other people like me.

_____15. Even if I am not enjoying myself, I often pretend to be having a good time.

_____16. I'm not always the person I appear to be.

_____17. I would not change my opinions (or the way I do things) in order to please someone else or win their favor.

_____18. I have considered being an entertainer.

_____19. In order to get along and be liked, I tend to be what people expect me to be rather than anything else.

_____20. I have never been good at games like charades or improvisational acting.

_____21. I have trouble changing my behavior to suit different people and different situations.

_____22. At a party, I let others keep the jokes and stories going.

_____23. I feel a bit awkward in company and do not show up quite so well as I should.

_____24. I can look anyone in the eye and tell a lie with a straight face (if for a right end).

_____25. I may deceive people by being friendly when I really dislike them.

SCORING THE SCALE

The scoring key is reproduced below. You should circle your response of true or false each time it corresponds to the keyed response below. Add up the number of responses you circle, and this total is your score on the Self-Monitoring Scale. Record your score below.

1. False	6. True	11. True	16. True	21. False
2. False	7. True	12. False	17. False	22. False
3. False	8. True	13. True	18. True	23. False
4. False	9. False	14. False	19. True	24. True
5. True	10. True	15. True	20. False	25. True

MY SCORE _____

WHAT THE SCALE MEASURES

Developed by Mark Snyder (1974), the Self-Monitoring (SM) Scale measures the extent to which you consciously employ impression management strategies in social interactions. Basically, the scale assesses the degree to which you manipulate the nonverbal signals that you send to others, and the degree to which you adjust your behavior to situational demands. As you know from Chapter 6 in your text, some people work harder at managing their public images than do others. The Self-Monitoring Scale measures how much attention you devote to this endeavor. A critical element in this process involves carefully controlling your non-verbal communication, which usually is pretty spontaneous (see Chapter 7 in your text).

RESEARCH ON THE SCALE

In his original study, Snyder (1974) reported very reasonable test-retest reliability (.83 for one month) and, for an initial study, provided ample evidence regarding the scale's validity. In assessing the validity of the scale, he found that in comparison to low SM subjects, high SM subjects were rated (by peers) as being better at emotional self-control and better at figuring out how to behave appropriately in new social situations. High SM subjects were also found to be superior on a nonverbal communication task. Furthermore, Snyder found that stage actors tended to score higher on the scale than undergraduates, as one would expect. Additionally, Ickes and Barnes (1977) summarize evidence that high SM people are: (1) very sensitive to situational cues, (2) particularly skilled at detecting deception on the part of others, and (3) especially insightful about how to influence the emotions of others.

INTERPRETING YOUR SCORE

Our norms are based on guidelines provided by Ickes and Barnes (1977) who did not spell out exactly how they arrived at their divisions regarding high, medium and low scores. The divisions are based on data from 207 undergraduate subjects.

Norms

High score:	15 - 22
Intermediate score:	9 - 14
Low score:	0 - 8

High scorers: A score in this range means that you devote a great deal of attention to carefully managing your self-presentations. You are quite concerned about behaving in ways that will be considered "appropriate" by others. You are sensitive to others' self-presentations and skillful at deciphering them. You are very aware of your nonverbal behavior and you try more than others to control it. You probably are talented at concealing emotions that you experience (when advantageous) and at portraying emotions that you think others want to see.

Intermediate scorers: A score in this category simply means that you display the characteristics described above to a moderate degree. In other words, you do a fair amount of self-monitoring but your concern about self-presentation is neither constant nor obsessive.

Low scorers: If you fall in this category, you pay relatively little attention to impression management. You do not worry particularly about creating the "right" image. You probably behave spontaneously and speak candidly. You do not change your behavior according to the nature of the social situation. In all likelihood, you are not very tuned into your own nonverbal behavior or that of others. Your emotions are expressed with relatively little "editing."

Name _____

Self-Expression (Assertiveness) Scale

For use with Chapters 7 or 8.

INSTRUCTIONS

The following inventory is designed to provide information about the way in which you express yourself. Please answer the questions by filling in the appropriate number from 0-4 (Almost Always or Always, 0; Usually, 1; Sometimes, 2; Seldom, 3; Never or Rarely, 4) next to each item. Your answer should reflect how you generally express yourself in the situation. If in responding to any of the questions you find that the situation described is not presently applicable to you - for example, you do not have a roommate - please do not skip the question. Instead, answer it in terms of how you think you would be likely to react if you were in the situation. Please do not skip any questions. Record your responses in the spaces provided on the left.

THE SCALE

_____ 1. Do you ignore it when someone pushes in front of you in line?

_____ 2. When you decide that you no longer wish to date someone, do you have marked difficulty telling the person of your decision?

_____ 3. Would you exchange a purchase you discover to be faulty?

_____ 4. If you decided to change your major to a field which your parents will not approve, would you have difficulty telling them?

_____ 5. Are you inclined to be over-apologetic?

_____ 6. If you were studying and if your roommate were making too much noise, would you ask him to stop?

_____ 7. Is it difficult for you to compliment and praise others?

_____ 8. If you are angry at your parents, can you tell them?

_____ 9. Do you insist that your roommate do his fair share of the cleaning?

_____ 10. If you find yourself becoming fond of someone you are dating, would you have difficulty expressing these feelings to that person?

_____11. If a friend who has borrowed $5.00 from you seems to have forgotten about it, would you remind this person?

_____12. Are you overly careful to avoid hurting other people's feelings?

_____13. If you have a close friend whom your parents dislike and constantly criticize, would you inform your parents that you disagree with them and tell them of your friend's assets?

_____14. Do you find it difficult to ask a friend to do a favor for you?

_____15. If food which is not to your satisfaction is served in a restaurant, would you complain about it to the waiter?

_____16. If your roommate without your permission eats food that he knows you have been saving, can you express your displeasure to him?

_____17. If a salesman has gone to considerable trouble to show you some merchandise which is not quite suitable, do you have difficulty saying no?

_____18. Do you keep your opinions to yourself?

_____19. If friends visit when you want to study, do you ask them to return at a more convenient time?

_____20. Are you able to express love and affection to people for whom you care?

_____21. If you were in a small seminar and the professor made a statement that you considered untrue, would you question it?

_____22. If a person of the opposite sex whom you have been wanting to meet smiles or directs attention to you at a party, would you take the initiative in beginning conversation?

_____23. If someone you respect expresses opinions with which you strongly disagree, would you venture to state your own point of view?

_____24. Do you go out of your way to avoid trouble with other people?

_____25. If a friend is wearing a new outfit which you like, do you tell that person so?

_____26. If after leaving a store you realize that you have been "short-changed," do you go back and request the correct amount?

_____27. If a friend makes what you consider to be an unreasonable request, are you able to refuse?

_____28. If a close and respected relative were annoying you, would you hide your feelings rather than express your annoyance?

_____29. If your parents want you to come home for a weekend but you have made important plans, would you tell them of your preference?

_____30. Do you express anger or annoyance toward the opposite sex when it is justified?

_____31. If a friend does an errand for you, do you tell that person how much you appreciate it?

_____32. When a person is blatantly unfair, do you fail to say something about it to him?

_____33. Do you avoid social contacts for fear of doing or saying the wrong thing?

_____34. If a friend betrays your confidence, would you hesitate to express annoyance to that person?

_____35. When a clerk in a store waits on someone who has come in after you, do you call his attention to the matter?

_____36. If you are particularly happy about someone's good fortune, can you express this to that person?

_____37. Would you be hesitant about asking a good friend to lend you a few dollars?

_____38. If a person teases you to the point that it is no longer fun, do you have difficulty expressing your displeasure?

_____39. If you arrive late for a meeting, would you rather stand than go to a front seat which could only be secured with a fair degree of conspicuousness?

_____40. If your date calls on Saturday night 15 minutes before you are supposed to meet and says that she (he) has to study for an important exam and cannot make it, would you express your annoyance?

_____41. If someone keeps kicking the back of your chair in a movie, would you ask him to stop?

_____42. If someone interrupts you in the middle of an important conversation, do you request that the person wait until you have finished?

_____43. Do you freely volunteer information or opinions in class discussions?

_____44. Are you reluctant to speak to an attractive acquaintance of the opposite sex?

_____45. If you lived in an apartment and the landlord failed to make certain necessary repairs after promising to do so, would you insist on it?

_____46. If your parents want you home by a certain time which you feel is much too early and unreasonable, do you attempt to discuss or negotiate this with them?

_____47. Do you find it difficult to stand up for your rights?

_____48. If a friend unjustifiably criticizes you, do you express your resentment there and then?

_____49. Do you express your feelings to others?

_____50. Do you avoid asking questions in class for fear of feeling self-conscious?

SCORING THE SCALE

In order to score this scale you have to reverse the number you entered for 29 of the items. The items to be reversed are listed below.

3	13	20	25	30	40	45
6	15	21	26	31	41	46
8	16	22	27	35	42	48
9	19	23	29	36	43	49
11						

For all of the items listed above you have to go back and make the following conversions.

If you entered 0 change it to 4.

If you entered 1 change it to 3.

If you entered 2 leave it at 2.

If you entered 3 change it to 1.

If you entered 4 change it to 0.

Now you simply add up all of the numbers for all 50 items, using the new numbers on the reversed items. This sum is your score on the College Self-expression Scale. Enter it below.

MY SCORE _____

WHAT THE SCALE MEASURES

The College Self-expression Scale (Galassi, Delo, Galassi & Bastien, 1974) is designed to measure assertiveness in college students. As explained in Chapter 8 of your text, assertiveness involves the degree to which people act in their own best interests by expressing their thoughts directly and honestly. In a nutshell, assertiveness constitutes the degree to which you stand up for your rights.

RESEARCH ON THE SCALE

Test-retest reliability over a two week period is quite high (Galassi et al., 1974). Validity was examined by correlating assertiveness scores with various scales from a widely used personality test called the Adjective Check List (Gough & Heilbrun, 1965). As predicted, assertiveness correlated positively with personality traits such as self-confidence, dominance and autonomy, while correlating negatively with traits such as abasement and deference (Galassi et al., 1974). Since it is important to distinguish between assertiveness and aggressiveness, the utility of the scale was enhanced by the fact that assertiveness scores did not correlate significantly with aggression scores on the Adjective Check List.

INTERPRETING YOUR SCORE

Our norms are based on a sizable sample, 1014 undergraduates at a major university. Although males scored a bit higher than females, the difference was not large enough to merit reporting separate norms by sex.

Norms

Assertive Score:	146-200	(more than 1 standard deviation above the mean)
Intermediate Score:	104-145	(within 1 standard deviation of the mean either way)
Non-assertive Score:	0-103	(more than 1 standard deviation below the mean)

Assertive Scorers: A score in this category suggests that you are rather consistently and strongly assertive. This means that you stand up for your rights when others try to infringe upon them. You are relatively unlikely to let people push you around or take advantage of you. You express your anger when it seems justified and you are able to turn down unreasonable requests.

Intermediate Scorers: A score in this range means that you are about average in assertiveness. While you are not passive or submissive, you are not exceptionally quick to stand up for your rights. You probably experience some discomfort in situations where you have to behave assertively. Nonetheless, you are capable of assertive behavior when the situation demands it.

Non-assertive Scorers: A score below 104 suggests that you have considerable difficulty in standing up for your rights. You probably tend to let others take advantage of you and you may have trouble saying "no" to unreasonable requests. You may also have a hard time expressing your disagreement with other people. In terms of personality traits, you may be bashful, meek, timid and inhibited. According to Galassi et al. (1974), you are a prime candidate for assertiveness training.

Name _____

Social Avoidance and Distress Scale

For use with Chapters 7 or 9.

INSTRUCTIONS

The statements below inquire about your personal reactions to a variety of situations. Consider each statement carefully. Then indicate whether the statement is true or false in regard to your typical behavior. Record your responses (true or false) in the spaces provided on the left.

THE SCALE

_____ 1. I feel relaxed even in unfamiliar social situations.

_____ 2. I try to avoid situations which force me to be very sociable.

_____ 3. It is easy for me to relax when I am with strangers.

_____ 4. I have no particular desire to avoid people.

_____ 5. I often find social occasions upsetting.

_____ 6. I usually feel calm and comfortable at social occasions.

_____ 7. I am usually at ease when talking to someone of the opposite sex.

_____ 8. I try to avoid talking to people unless I know them well.

_____ 9. If the chance comes to meet new people, I often take it.

_____ 10. I often feel nervous or tense in casual get-togethers in which both sexes are present.

_____ 11. I am usually nervous with people unless I know them well.

_____ 12. I usually feel relaxed when I am with a group of people.

_____ 13. I often want to get away from people.

_____ 14. I usually feel uncomfortable when I am in a group of people I don't know.

_____ 15. I usually feel relaxed when I meet someone for the first time.

_____ 16. Being introduced to people makes me tense and nervous.

_____ 17. Even though a room is full of strangers, I may enter it anyway.

_____ 18. I would avoid walking up and joining a large group of people.

_____ 19. When my superiors want to talk with me, I talk willingly.

_____ 20. I often feel on edge when I am with a group of people.

_____ 21. I tend to withdraw from people.

_____ 22. I don't mind talking to people at parties or social gatherings.

_____ 23. I am seldom at ease in a large group of people.

_____ 24. I often think up excuses in order to avoid social engagements.

_____ 25. I sometimes take the responsibility for introducing people to each other.

_____ 26. I try to avoid formal social occasions.

_____ 27. I usually go to whatever social engagements I have.

_____ 28. I find it easy to relax with other people.

SCORING THE SCALE

The scoring key is reproduced below. You should circle your true or false response each time it corresponds to the keyed response below. Add up the number of responses you circle, and this total is your score on the SAD scale. Record your score below.

1.	False	8.	True	15.	False	22.	False
2.	True	9.	False	16.	True	23.	True
3.	False	10.	True	17.	False	24.	True
4.	False	11.	True	18.	True	25.	False
5.	True	12.	False	19.	False	26.	True
6.	False	13.	True	20.	True	27.	False
7.	False	14.	True	21.	True	28.	False

MY SCORE _____

WHAT THE SCALE MEASURES

As its name implies, this scale measures social avoidance and distress in social interactions. David Watson and Ronald Friend (1969) developed the scale to assess the extent to which individuals experience discomfort, fear and anxiety in social situations and the extent to which they therefore attempt to evade many kinds of social encounters. Essentially, the scale measures a couple of aspects of excessive caution in interpersonal relations -- a condition discussed in your text in Chapter 9 under shyness.

RESEARCH ON THE SCALE

Watson and Friend (1969) report very satisfactory estimates of internal reliability and review convincing evidence that the scale is not unduly contaminated by social desirability bias. To check the validity of the scale, they used it to predict subjects' social behavior in experimentally contrived situations. As projected, they found that people who scored high on the SAD scale were less willing than low scorers to participate in a group discussion. The high scorers also reported anticipating more anxiety about their participation in the discussion than did the low scorers. Additionally, Watson and Friend found a strong negative correlation (-.76) between the SAD and a measure of affiliation drive.

INTERPRETING YOUR SCORE

Our norms are based on data collected by Watson and Friend (1969) on over 200 university students. The preponderance of people score relatively low on the scale, as you can see from the norms below.

Norms

High Score:	16-28	(more than 0.75 standard deviations above the mean)
Intermediate Score:	6-15	(from 0.50 standard deviations below the mean up to 0.75 standard deviations above the mean)
Low Score:	0-5	(more than 0.50 standard deviations below the mean)

High Scorers: A high score on the SAD scale means that you report considerable distress about a variety of social situations and probably go out of your way to avoid many of these situations. To put it more bluntly, you are probably above average in shyness. A high score suggests that you may be timid, reticent and very self-conscious in dealing with people other than those who you know very well.

Intermediate Scorers: A score in this range indicates that you have a moderate amount of social anxiety. As discussed in your text (see Chapter 9), research indicates that shyness is situational for most people. Thus, your score probably means that you are socially anxious in some situations but not others.

Low Scorers: A low score means that you generally do not experience tension and anxiety in social interactions. Watson and Friend emphasize that this does not mean that you are necessarily extraverted, outgoing and socially aggressive. It only means that you do not feel threatened when socializing with new people. Instead, you feel calm, relaxed and comfortable when dealing with others.

Test-Wiseness Scale

For use with Chapter 12

INSTRUCTIONS

Below you will find a series of 24 history questions for which you are not expected to know the answer based on your knowledge of history. However, you should be able to make a good guess on each of the questions if you can spot the flaws that exist in every item. Each question is flawed in some way so as to permit solution by test-wise examinees. Record your choice for each question in the spaces provided on the left.

THE SCALE

_____ 1. The Locarno Pact:
   a. is an international agreement for the maintenance of peace through the guarantee of national boundaries of France, Germany, Italy, Belgium and other countries of Western Europe
   b. allowed France to occupy the Ruhr Valley
   c. provided for the dismemberment of Austria-Hungary
   d. provided for the protection of Red Cross bases during war times

_____ 2. The disputed Hayes-Tilden election of 1876 was settled by an
   a. resolution of the House of Representatives
   b. decision of United States Supreme Court
   c. Electoral Commission
   d. joint resolution of Congress

_____ 3. The Factory Act of 1833 made new provisions for the inspection of the mills. This new arrangement was important because:
   a. the inspectors were not local men and therefore they had no local ties which might affect the carrying out of their job; they were responsible to the national government rather than to the local authorities, and they were encouraged to develop a professional skill in handling their work
   b. the inspectorate was recruited from the factory workers
   c. the inspectors were asked to recommend new legislation
   d. the establishment of the factory inspectorate gave employment to large numbers of the educated middle class

_____ 4. The Ostend Manifesto aimed to
    a. discourage Southern expansionism
    b. prevent expansion in the South
    c. aid Southern expansionism
    d. all of the above

_____ 5. The august character of the work of Pericles in Athens frequently causes his work to be likened to that in Rome of:
    a. Augustus
    b. Sulla
    c. Pompey
    d. Claudius

_____ 6. The Webster-Ashburton Treaty settled a long-standing dispute between Great Britain and the United States over:
    a. the Maine boundary
    b. numerous contested claims to property as well as many other sources of ill-will
    c. damages growing out of the War of 1812 and subsequent events
    d. fishing rights on the Great Lakes and in international waters

_____ 7. Men who opposed the "Ten Hour Movement" in British factory history:
    a. was a leader in the dominant political party
    b. is convinced that shorter hours of work are bad for the morals of the laboring classes
    c. is primarily motivated by concern for his own profits
    d. were convinced that intervention would endanger the economic welfare of Britain

_____ 8. The career of Marius (155-86 B.C.), the opponent of Sulla, is significant in Roman history because
    a. he gave many outstanding dinners and entertainments for royalty
    b. he succeeded in arming the gladiators
    c. he showed that the civil authority could be thrust aside by the military
    d. he made it possible for the popular party to conduct party rallies outside the city of Rome

_____ 9. The Locarno Pact
    a. was an agreement between Greece and Turkey
    b. gave the Tyrol to Italy
    c. was a conspiracy to blow up the League of Nations' building at Locarno
    d. guaranteed the boundary arrangements in Western Europe

_____ 10. The first Presidential election dispute in the United States to be settled by an appointed Electoral Commission was
    a. the Hayes-Tilden election
    b. the Jefferson-Madison election
    c. the John Quincy Adams-Henry Clay election
    d. the Garfield-McKinley election

_____11. The first of the alliances against the "Central Powers" which ended in World War I is to be found in
    a. the defensive treaty between China and Japan
    b. the dual alliance of Mexico and the United States
    c. the dual alliance of France and Russia
    d. India's resentment against South Africa's attitude toward the Boer War, and her ensuing alliance with Japan

_____12. The Proclamation of 1763
    a. forbade colonists to settle territory acquired in the French and Indian wars
    b. encouraged colonists to settle territory acquired in the French and Indian wars
    c. provided financial incentives for settlement of territory acquired in the French and Indian wars
    d. all of the above

_____13. About what fraction of the 1920 population of the United States was foreign-born?
    a. less than five per cent
    b. between fourteen and twenty-eight per cent
    c. twenty-five percent
    d. between thirty and fifty per cent

_____14. The Alabama claims were
    a. all settled completely and satisfactorily
    b. claims against Jefferson Davis for seizure of all of the property in the state during wartime
    c. claims of the United States against Great Britain
    d. claims of every citizen of Alabama against every citizen of Georgia

_____15. During the Italian Renaissance
    a. the papacy gained political power
    b. there were frequent changes in government
    c. the papacy became more important in Italian political affairs
    d. all of the above

_____16. The 12th Century was distinguished by a 'real European patriotism' which expressed itself in
    a. the flowering of lyrical and epical poetry in the vernacular
    b. great patriotic loyalty to the undivided unit of European Christendom
    c. recurring attempts to form a world with a centralized administration
    d. proposals to remove the custom barriers between the different countries of the time

_____17. The dispute between Great Britain and the United States over the boundary of Maine was settled by
    a. the Treaty of Quebec
    b. the Treaty of Niagara
    c. the Webster-Ashburton Treaty
    d. the Pendleton-Scott Treaty

_____18. In the Dartmouth College case the United States Supreme Court held
    a. that the courts had no right under any circumstance ever to nullify an Act of Congress
    b. that a state could not impair a contract
    c. all contracts must be agreeable to the state legislature
    d. that all contracts must inevitably be certified

_____19. The accessions of Henry VII marked the close of the
    a. Crusades
    b. War of the Roses, between rival factions of the English nobility
    c. Hundred Years' War
    d. Peasants' Revolt

_____20. The Magna Charta was signed
    a. before the Norman invasion
    b. in 1215
    c. after the opening of the 17th Century
    d. about the middle of the 14th Century

_____21. The Progressive Party in 1912
    a. favored complete protective tariffs
    b. favored an appointed Congress
    c. favored the creation of a non-partisan tariff commission
    d. favored restriction of the ballot to certain influential persons

_____22. The first systematic attempt to establish the Alexandrian synthesis between Christian religious belief and Greek civilization was undertaken at
    a. Rome
    b. Alexandria
    c. Athens
    d. Jerusalem

_____23. The Bland-Allison Act
    a. made all forms of money redeemable in silver
    b. standardized all gold dollars in terms of silver and copper
    c. made none of the paper money redeemable in silver
    d. directed the Treasury Department to purchase a certain amount of silver bullion each month

_____24. The famed Bayeaux Tapestry is a
    a. enormous re-creation of the Magna Charta scene
    b. extremely large impression of the Edict of Nantes
    c. immense picture of the Battle of Tours
    d. large representation of the Norman Conquest of England

SCORING THE SCALE

There are eight item-writing flaws which appear on the Test-Wiseness Scale (TWS) three times each. They are described below. Your text elaborates on these flaws in the Application section of Chapter 12.

Flaw #1:   The incorrect options are highly implausible.

Flaw #2:   Equivalence and/or contradictions among options allows one to eliminate the incorrect options.

Flaw #3:   Content information in other items provides the answer.

Flaw #4:   The correct option is more detailed and specific than all the other options.

Flaw #5:   The correct option is consistently longer than all of the other options.

Flaw #6:   There is grammatical inconsistency between the stem and the incorrect options but not the correct option.

Flaw #7:   The incorrect options include certain key words that tend to appear in false statements (such as always, must, never and so on).

Flaw #8:   There is a resemblance between the stem and the correct option but not the incorrect options.

The scoring key is reproduced below. For each item it tells you the correct answer, and indicates which flaw (as numbered above) you should have spotted to arrive at the answer. Circle those items that you got correct. Add up the number of correct items and that is your score on the Test-Wiseness Scale. Record your score below.

1. A (5)	7. D (6)	13. C (4)	19. B (5)
2. C (6)	8. C (1)	14. C (7)	20. B (4)
3. A (5)	9. D (3)	15. D (2)	21. C (1)
4. C (2)	10. A (3)	16. B (8)	22. B (8)
5. A (8)	11. C (1)	17. C (3)	23. D (7)
6. A (4)	12. A (2)	18. B (7)	24. D (6)

MY SCORE _____

WHAT THE SCALE MEASURES

As its title indicates, this scale simply measures your ability at reasoning your way to answers on multiple choice exams. The Test-Wiseness Scale assesses test-taking skills.

RESEARCH ON THE SCALE

The Test-Wiseness Scale you just took is an abbreviated version of a scale developed by your author. Although the scale has been used in research (Weiten, Clery & Bowbin, 1980) it has not yet been formally published as it is still undergoing refinement. The full scale is a 40-item test with five items for each kind of flaw. Due to space limitations I eliminated (randomly) two items for each flaw type to reduce the scale to 24 questions.

The TWS is built on some pioneering work by Gibb (1964). Through a series of revisions, reliability, validity and item discrimination have gradually been improved. The present version (full-length) yields internal reliability coefficients in the .70's and .80's. Two lines of evidence currently provide support for the scale's validity (additional validation studies are underway). First, it has been found that scores on the scale are very much affected (positively) by training in the principles of test-wiseness. Second, as one would expect, the scale correlates positively (.40s) with classroom performance on multiple-choice tests. More importantly, this correlation between the TWS and classroom performance remains significant even when the influence of intelligence on both variables is factored out statistically (with a partial correlation).

INTERPRETING YOUR SCORE

Our norms are based on the performance of 76 undergraduates who took the most recent revision of the scale. These norms are for people who have not had any test-wiseness training. If you have carefully read the Application section of Chapter 12 in your text, you should expect to get a score in or near the high range.

Norms

High score:	17 - 24	(more than 1 standard deviation above the mean)
Intermediate score:	9 - 16	(within 1 standard deviation of the mean either way)
Low score:	0 - 8	(more than 1 standard deviation below the mean)

High scorers: A score in this range means you are substantially above average in test-wiseness. This bodes well for your academic future. It means that you know how to take advantage of clues that frequently exist in multiple-choice tests. It also means that you can "think on your feet" when taking an examination; you can reason your way to a plausible answer even when you're not sure. Above all else, it means that you're skilled at taking tests.

Intermediate scorers: A score in this bracket means that you are roughly average in test-wiseness. This suggests that there is room for improvement. You might want to think about looking at a book or article (see your text for suggestions) on how to enhance your test-taking capabilities.

Low scorers: A score in this category suggests that you are not very good at taking multiple-choice tests. It would almost certainly be wise to pursue additional information that might help you to become more skilled on tests.